Essay Index

all Cops

POLITICS AND LITERATURE
IN MODERN BRITAIN

POLITICS AND LITERATURE IN MODERN BRITAIN

GEORGE WATSON

ROWMAN AND LITTLEFIELD

Totowa, New Jersey

First published in the United States 1977 by
ROWMAN AND LITTLEFIELD, Totowa, N.J.

First published in the United Kingdom 1977 by
The Macmillan Press Ltd

Library of Congress Cataloging in Publication Data

Watson, George, 1927–
    Politics and literature in modern Britain.

    Includes bibliographical references and index.
    1. English Literature—20th century—History and
criticism. 2. Politics and literature. 3. English
literature—19th century—History and criticism.
I. Title.
PR479.P6W3   820′.9′31   77–4664
ISBN 0–87471–987–9

PRINTED IN GREAT BRITAIN

Contents

Acknowledgements

A surprising number of editors and academic hosts encouraged me to deliver or publish these essays in more primitive and unreflected forms; and a good many outspoken friends, among others, have since helped me to embellish them. My gratitude to them all is wide and deep. 'The New Left' was delivered as the St John's College, Cambridge lecture at the University of Hull in March 1975; and 'Race and the Socialists' as the Elliott Dodds lecture at the University of Leeds in November 1975. Both have since appeared in *Encounter*, that mouthpiece of passionate moderation, as well as 'Did Stalin Dupe the Intellectuals?' and 'The Politics of D. H. Lawrence'. 'George Orwell' first saw the light of print in the *Journal of European Studies*, 'The Literature of Fascism' in the *Lugano Review*, 'The Myth of Catastrophe' in the *Yale Review*, and 'The Social Criticism of Matthew Arnold' in the *Review of English Literature*; but all are altered here, and many enlarged. Others are new.

My thanks are due to the Leverhulme Trust for help in working on the Acton manuscripts, and to the Rockefeller Foundation for time to write and rewrite in the Villa Serbelloni; to the Librarian of the House of Commons for sympathetic guidance; to the historical seminar on the Victorians and their successors conducted over the years by Dr Henry Pelling and the late George Kitson Clark at Cambridge, where my Arnold paper and 'Left and Right' were first exposed to the light and air of professional criticism; and to members of the Unservile State Group, to whom this book is irresistibly dedicated, for the stimulus of their advice over a quarter-century.

St John's College, Cambridge   G. W.

Introduction

These essays are arranged in chronological order from present to past, from the mid-twentieth century back into the mid-Victorian period, or from the more familiar towards the less. That is perhaps the best order in which to read them. On the other hand, they stand independently of each other. They are about political literature in Britain in the last hundred years, and the political views and influence of men of letters. Designed from the start as a book, they are unlikely to suffer from disunity of purpose, and I am concerned here to uphold the independence of each part; not to enforce a merger but to encourage each essay to stand on its feet and speak for itself.

The book represents a sequel to *The English Ideology* (1973), a study of Victorian political language. But the compass of the present book, which is similar in its assumptions, is much wider: political literature since the 1860s, when the Second Reform Act of 1867 and the first Liberal government in Britain, formed by Gladstone in the following year, plainly heralded a new era. Arnold's *Culture and Anarchy* (1869) was to follow a year later: an anti-Gladstonian tract by an established poet and critic of the age; and Lord Acton began his 'History of Liberty' soon after as a Gladstonian manifesto. Since the 1860s Britain has richly experienced all the rewards and trials of an industrial–democratic state: trials and rewards by now familiar enough elsewhere, but played out in Britain in the remarkable context of an advanced literary culture.

Intellectual history is a risk-laden enterprise, especially since it often straddles more academic interests than one. I write here as a literary historian intruding on the open preserves of political and social history; but some early warnings may lessen the risks and set these essays in a clearer perspective. I offer the following observations to explain and justify my own interpretations of political thought. If they could be seen as axioms, so much the better; an ideal reader would probably see them as truisms, and wonder why they should need to be set out at all.

1. In the progress of political ideas, originality happens. The historian seeks out sources where they exist; but an analogue is not a source, however revealing, and I have tried to keep a mind hospitable to the notion that a poet, novelist or polemicist may have conceived of a political idea for himself.

2. Literature makes assertions – whether as poems, plays or novels, essays or treatises – and about politics, among other things. And it matters what it asserts and whether it is true or false. That is not to imply that works of literature are good to the extent that they are true, or bad to the extent that they are false, and the one view does not entail the other. But it is one of the least impressive pea-and-thimble tricks of formalist critics to pretend that literature is always a way of seeing, never a thing seen; or that a poet or novelist always speaks in the voice of a dramatic narrator, never his own; or, for that matter, that the voice of a dramatic character in a play or novel cannot also be the author's own. Literature often has persuasive intent and persuasive force. It can even be propaganda. To deny that is to deny much in the ordinary experience of reading and writing, and to exchange some of the life-and-death anxieties of the human mind for a fribble.

3. Considered as a descriptive instrument, all language is in a state of dilapidation. T. S. Eliot once called it 'shabby equipment always deteriorating'. That is because it is inherited from situations unlike the present. Since political realities shift faster than most, this dilapidation is exceptionally damaging in the sphere of political description. Would any twentieth-century European, if he had not inherited from the nineteenth such terms as Left and Right, or working class and middle class, imagine for a moment that such terms describe the political and social realities in which he lives? 'The Isms are all *Wasms*', somebody wittily remarked at the Foreign Office in August 1939, when a pact of friendship was announced between Hitler and Stalin. But then, Isms usually are Wasms: it is just that it takes a jolt of history to make men see it. The socialist countries to-day operate a state capitalism more total than the Pharaohs', and far more total than Elizabeth I's state monopolies; and yet millions who do not have to live in them think them left-wing.

The alternative of devising a new political language, for all that, remains awesome. For one thing, it would mean looking harder – and much harder than the most alert among us are accustomed to – at the political realities that surround us. For another, it would mean enduring, and probably for no short period, the incomprehension of others. It is entirely understandable for both these reasons that much political language remains clumsily and misleadingly conservative, and at least as much so in the mouths of radicals as of conservatives. But political terms fortunately die, if all too slowly; and perhaps the sensible limits of intelligent ambition here would be to encourage them to die a little faster. We might choose to talk of rank rather than of class, for instance, since rank is a descriptively subtler tool for depicting social differences; and now that the political choices of Europe are more clearly about liberty than at any time since the French revolutionary wars, we might resolve to speak less often of Left and Right, and more of liberal and illiberal.

4. Language, for better or worse, can make reality; and what men believe can become true for no better reason than that they think in such terms as they do. No one, it has been said, would ever fall in love if the phrase did not exist. Dilapidated as our political language is, there is a continuous threat that reality might come to reflect it all too accurately by dint of imitating it. Political language keeps its terrible power for as long as it is thought to perform accurately as a descriptive instrument; and one can help it to die only by exposing its inaccuracies. But that contest, in the end, has something of the simplicity of a race between two teams: if its inaccuracy is not soon exposed, it can all too easily cease to be that and turn true. In the present century of mankind, and for the first time in human history, utopia can happen, and the books men wrote in the Reading-Room of the British Museum or in a Bavarian prison may become real. If all that is to be frustrated, it can only be by the unremitting arguments of clear-headed and fervent minds.

5. Old men forget, and so do the middle-aged. What is worse, they sometimes remember creatively, attributing to their youth views they later wished they had held when young. For that reason, only documentary evidence dating from youth itself is clear evidence of the convictions of youth. An author is often a poor and unreliable witness to his own early opinions.

6. Eye-witnesses too can give uncertain evidence. Proust's character Madame de Villeparisis, when famous writers were men-

tioned in company, was fond of saying: 'I know I can speak about that, because they used to visit my father; and as Mr Sainte-Beuve used to say (and he was very intelligent), one must believe those who have seen things at close hand. . . .' The best use for the eye-witness is to create in one's mind a sense of period. But the witness can easily suffer from the over-confidence of the man who was there; and he is often convinced, and rightly, that his own interpretations or mis-interpretations will be held to count for more than those of the patient historian who has raked the periodicals and hunted out the manuscripts. Every historian of the contemporary and near-contem-porary must be haunted by the thought of a Madame de Villeparisis.

7. Intellectual history is about what men have *said*, in speech or in writing. The verbs 'to think' and 'to believe' are too convenient to be avoided here, but they are not in this context to be regarded literally: what men have silently thought or believed is not the object of the enquiry. This is a history of public events, in the sense that speaking and writing are public. That is why the defence of insincerity, even when true, is beside the point. 'Yes, I suppose I did say or write that, but it wasn't what I really believed. . . .' But what men have 'really' believed, in that context, is not the game the historian is hunting. His retort is all too obvious: 'Then you shouldn't have said it.' And those who emphasise that there are many kinds of belief sometimes need to be reminded that no kind of belief can without sophistry be seen as a kind of disbelief.

Men are responsible for what they say or write, then, whether in full sincerity or not. Whatever political influence men of letters possess, for good or ill, this daunting conclusion may help to join it, if belatedly, to a sense of responsibility.

8. People often hold contradictory views. To suppose, then, that a man who believed X cannot also have believed Y, where X and Y are in contradiction, and solely on the ground that they are in con-tradiction, is to exceed the evidence. 'Inconsistencies cannot both be right,' as Johnson remarks in *Rasselas,* 'but imputed to man they may both be true'.

9. 'Rulers crumble, thinkers reign', Acton once observed. In the realm of politics, opinion governs behaviour, and this conviction is fundamental to anyone seriously concerned with the history of political thought. Two kinds of sceptic are inclined to deny it: those who understand 'opinion' in an excessively restricted sense; and determinists of one sort or another. But opinion represents

something wider here than idealism or ideology: it includes self-interest, for example – as a statesman who accepts a bribe might be said to have acted on an opinion about the importance of being rich. As for determinism, it has tended in the present century to be either psychological or social. But psychological determinism does little here except alter the rhetoric of debate, and rarely for the better: an explanation in psychological terms of why a man holds a view does not annul the fact that he holds it. And broadly similar objections apply to theories of social conditioning: it is profoundly irrelevant, even when it is true, to insist that an author believes what he does because he was socially conditioned into believing it. The same strictures apply to wilder and woollier versions of the sociology of thought, whether class-determination or structures of feeling. The real interest of an idea is forever intrinsic. It is not *why* a conviction was held that is of the first significance in this enquiry, but what that conviction was.

1 | *The New Left*

The literary sources of the British New Left make a conveniently modest subject for the historian. Britain was never exactly pre-eminent in this field: the New Left from the start was international, its German roots spreading rapidly outwards into France and America. Its chief flowering was in the United States in the 1960s; its noisiest and most hectic existence was lived out in the great mass-universities of North America and the European Continent, and rarely in the shy, selective backwaters of British academic life.

Modest, too, in the time-scale. As an active and visible movement the New Left lasted internationally for less than a decade, from the California of 1964 to the withdrawal of American troops from Indo-China in 1971–2. In the ancient traditions of Marxism, a faith now well over a century old, this is little more than a bubble on the ocean surface. One might even argue, in a reasonable if hardfaced sort of way, that in real terms the New Left never amounted to much, and that the Marxists who really matter are those who govern one-third of the human race and want to govern the rest. In the British context, that means those who take themselves to where power is: not to universities but to Parliament, the party-machines or the rich and vital power-points of the trade-union movement.

Such arguments should fail to daunt the literary historian precisely because they are true. A subject is all the more inviting for being delimited, and the literary sources of the New Left, in any case, make a strong appeal to the historical temper. They are themselves, after all, historiographical documents. Few political movements in recent times have been so deeply obsessed with the past as this. Mass political parties usually have very short memories: it is even difficult in a general election to maintain the interest of voters in the events of the Parliament just dissolved. But then the temper of popular politics is very unacademic; and the New Left was always strenuously academic, firmly chained in its arguments to an established scripture. Its sacred writings were the early papers of Marx, notably the Paris manuscripts of 1844, with their modern commentaries.[1] From the start it was committed to a traditional nineteenth-century dogma that 'capitalism' must inevitably give way to 'socialism' – a view which, since the 1950s, has been considered even in the Soviet Union to have been outmoded by events. It accepted unquestioningly, and from the start, the spectrum-view of political opinion as a struggle between Left and Right. In Britain its literary texts, like Richard Hoggart's *The Uses of Literacy* (1957) and Raymond Williams's *Culture and Society 1780–1950* (1958), were essentially retrospective studies of nineteenth- and early twentieth-century Britain. Any university teacher active in the Sixties will recall how colleagues and students of that persuasion commonly chose literary and historical studies within the period stretching from the 1830s to the First World War. The cult-figures, at least among native Britons, were such men as Carlyle, William Morris, Ruskin and Keir Hardie. This was always a neo-Victorian enthusiasm, and it is no wonder if it revived a fashion for beards.

What is more, the New Left was from the start intensely conscious of its own history. When I was in Berkeley in the late autumn of 1964, at the University of California, demonstrators often handed out leaflets that included long chronologies listing the day-by-day evolution of protest over the recent months: how the university had forbidden the sale of political literature on one day, how the partisans of free speech had reacted on the next, and how the academic authorities had responded to that. . . . The self-importance of the New Left, always considerable, was from the start historically self-conscious. It behaved as if future historians, and historians not far in the future at that, must one day raise their pens and write about it. Its auto-intoxication was archival. He who controls the past controls the future, as the rulers of Orwell's 1984 believed. The New Left went further than that: it sought to control its own history as it went. But it is itself, by now, a fact of the past, and he who controls its history may hope to control it.

★

Let me now attempt a brief backward view of the immediate literary sources of the British New Left.

The *New Left Review* began to appear in January 1960, incorporating the Oxford journal *Universities and Left Review* (1957–9) and the *New Reasoner* (1957–9), both of them dissident Communist journals emerging from the break-up of official communism in the West after the Soviet invasion of Hungary in October 1956, and the rise of the Campaign for Nuclear Disarmament in 1957–8. The editor of the *New Left Review* was Stuart Hall, a young Oxford graduate, and its first editorial board included Doris Lessing, Alasdair MacIntyre, Ralph Miliband, Edward Thompson and Raymond Williams – all academics, or academics-to-be, apart from Mrs Lessing the novelist. In its first editorial it struck a note of utopian socialism hostile to both Western consumerism and Soviet brutality, and Victorian sources were promptly invoked: 'The humanist strength of socialism . . . must be developed in cultural and social terms, as well as economic and political'; the editor beginning and ending his manifesto with sonorous quotations from William Morris, exclaiming 'How close Morris came to the bone!' In the same year the series 'New Left Books' was launched, its first volume being *Out of Apathy* (1960) by Edward Thompson and others.

The literary foundations of the New Left in Britain lie further back than 1960, but not much. A little spate of academic books of the Fifties herald the approach: Hoggart and Williams in 1957–8; studies of the English Civil War by Christopher Hill, who left the Communist Party over Hungary and who, as an historian, escaped the usual socialist obsession with the Victorians; and Edward Thompson's *The Making of the English Working Class*, a substantial study that did not appear until 1963. All this is more or less academic historiography, though *The Uses of Literacy,* which is several books worked into one, also smacks of autobiography and popular sociology. The intellectual leadership of the New Left in Britain was overwhelmingly a movement of academic historians, and after the first years there are few plays, poems or novels to add to the chronicle. Doris Lessing was not a political novelist for long, whatever her continuing convictions. The first of John Osborne's plays to be produced in the West End of London, *Look Back in Anger*, opened at the Royal Court Theatre in May 1956, months before the double trauma of the invasion of Hungary and the Suez War. The mood of its first act offered a vivid prediction of the New Left, then still unborn; and his next play, *The Entertainer* (1957), confirmed that mood. But Osborne shifted rapidly from the Left in the Sixties, and his later plays occupy no easily definable place on the political map; while Arnold Wesker, whose early plays *Roots* (1959) and *I'm Talking about Jerusalem* (1960) chime in with the mood of early Osborne, has since failed to hold a successful place in the London theatre. And the poems of Christopher Logue and Adrian Mitchell hang lightly in the balance.

In the wider field of cultural journalism, however, the New Left was more lastingly effective, both in periodicals and in paperbacks. The theatre criticism of Kenneth Tynan, the most influential dramatic critic in London from the early Fifties down to his appointment in 1963 as Literary Manager of the new National Theatre, gave massive journalistic support. Tynan had turned Brechtian with startling rapidity a few years after coming down from Oxford, after an early career dedicated to Noel Coward and Terence Rattigan. In 1955–6, reviewing productions of Brecht in Paris and London, he conceived German Epic Theatre to be the harsh medicine the West End needed to purge it of triviality, though on fashionable rather than dogmatic grounds: 'Unless we learn it soon, a familiar process will take place and the future of the theatre may have been strangled in its cot', he wrote in 1956,[2] and in a review of the same year he helped Osborne towards his resounding success. But the future will not hesitate to conclude that the New Left, as a sustained literary phenomenon, stands or falls as a kind of history and as a way of reading the past. Its contribution to fiction, poetry and the drama was lively for an instant, but too shortlived to count for much or for long.

This study, then, amounts to an obituary or autopsy on a school of history. In the worldly sense, it was a highly successful school. Some of its books sold massively enough to enrich their authors and to pitchfork them with notable suddenness into posts of enviable emolument. The New Left will some day deserve to be studied in these terms, when the accounts are opened and the wills are read; but it may already be hailed as an outstandingly successful event in consumer-appeal and a classic instance of advertising acumen. That, to be sure, may from the start have been among its objectives. But it cannot realistically have been its expectation, and its overtures were mournful. Both *The Uses of Literacy* and *Culture and Society* are pervaded by a sense of sorrowful nostalgia for a lost Europe when socialism once looked like a reasonable hope for intelligent men. These are sad, backward-looking books, obsessed with the 'residual

values' of a dying system of belief and with the daunting task, after
the collapse of such high hopes, of saving something or other from a
doctrinal wreck. Either could have served as well as an epitaph on
the Old Left as a clarion call to a New. Publishers and authors alike
are said to have been taken unawares by their success: the current of
intellectual socialist revivalism was running stronger and deeper
than anyone then guessed, and it was about to be propelled faster
and harder still by events themselves. 'There is not much
enthusiasm abroad among intellectuals in our time', wrote one of the
contributors to *Out of Apathy* in 1960, in sorrowing vein, 'for the day
when the last king will be strangled with the entrails of the last
priest'.[3] That sentence would not have been possible five or ten
years later. In 1960, ideology was widely supposed to be dead, a victim of a triumphant consumer society, and the drum-beats of the
Thirties were thought forever stilled by the final and unforgivable
Soviet apostasy at Budapest. The men of 1960 were building on a
ruin, and knew it. And yet the ruin proved a foundation, after all,
and on it they built.

★

Who were they? The evidence is not yet available to draw more than
a sketch of the principal sages of the New Left in the Britain of the
Sixties. But a social comparison with the only other generation of
British literary Marxists – Auden, Day Lewis, Spender, Isherwood
and their contemporaries in the Thirties – could prove enlightening.

The literary Marxist of the Thirties had been born in the first
decade of the century of professional parents, and his education was
almost always public school and Oxford or Cambridge. The New
Left sage, by contrast, was born in the second decade or soon after,
most often between the peace of 1918 and the General Strike of 1926.
Mr Christopher Hill, who in 1965 became Master of Balliol, falls
somewhat outside this pattern: he was born in 1912, which means
that he was easily old enough to share in the political enthusiasms of
the Spanish Civil War in 1936; he is a between-generations man.
Hoggart was born in 1918, Williams in 1921, Thompson in 1924.
Their parentage, as a group, is usually assumed to have been
'working-class'; this is not always true, but it remains true that it
was often socially inferior to that of the typical Thirties intellectual.
Hill is the son of a Methodist solicitor in York, and attended St

Peter's School there and then Balliol; Hoggart is the son of poor parents in Leeds who died when he was young, according to his own minutely circumstantial account in *The Uses of Literacy,* an account never seriously questioned; he attended local schools and in 1936 the University of Leeds. In 1939 he was accepted to read English at Cambridge, but was diverted by the war, in which he served as an officer. Williams was the son of a Monmouthshire railway signalman; he attended Abergavenny Grammar School, a Henry VIII foundation and at that time one of the few voluntary-aided schools in Wales, and then Trinity College, Cambridge, after which he too served as an officer in the war, returning later to complete his Cambridge degree. Edward Thompson, though younger than these, has an upbringing more like that of the older generation of Marxist intellectuals: his father had been a Methodist missionary in India who returned to England in 1923 to resign his ministry and live near Oxford, speaking and writing in favour of Indian independence; and his brother Frank was an active Communist until his death among the Bulgarian partisans in 1944.[4] Edward Thompson was schooled at Kingswood; he went from there to Cambridge to read history, joined the Communist Party as an undergraduate in 1942, went to war, finished his degree after the war and worked on a Yugoslav railway before the Stalin–Tito split of 1948.

The pattern of behaviour grows still clearer in adulthood, and it is a highly academic pattern. Hill became a Fellow of Balliol in 1938, after brief periods at All Souls (1934) and University College, Cardiff (1936). Hoggart, his war service over, became a staff tutor at Hull (1946–59) and later taught at the universities of Leicester (1959–62) and Birmingham (1962–70), to become an Assistant Director of UNESCO in Paris in 1970 and eventually principal of a London college. Williams, who completed his degree at Cambridge after the war, joined the Oxford University Extra-Mural Department in 1946 and became a lecturer in English at Cambridge in 1961, and later a professor and faculty chairman. Thompson was an extra-mural lecturer at Leeds from 1948 to 1965 and later a Reader in History at the new University of Warwick, from which he soon resigned to write *Warwick University Ltd* (1970), attacking the industrial connections of the new foundation and defending the student occupation of its registry in February 1970 to examine its 'secret files'.

The pattern is more than academic. It shows a marked tendency towards authorship and public appearance rather than the routine of teaching, and above all a profound attraction towards the mass media. Hoggart served on the Pilkington Committee on Broadcasting in 1960–2 which advocated a bigger role for the public sector in television in defiance of commercial interests; Williams edited the *May Day Manifesto* (1967, revised and enlarged 1968), drafted by a group first meeting in the summer of 1966. The university is often the base for activity, but rarely the activity itself, and the sage does not confine his energies to his own students when he has a whole nation to teach. If he is not rapidly promoted by his university, or if he reaches the limits of promotion, he may rapidly leave it. Egalitarianism is a political ideal here, but it has nothing to do with private behaviour. The career of the New Left sage is marked by an intense consciousness of worldly success, a high competitive drive worthy of the best capitalistic entrepreneur, and a quietly affluent life-style.

A faint yet self-conscious ambiguity hangs over his social origins. A published conversation between Hoggart and Williams in the first number of the *New Left Review* (January–February 1960) touches on the matter with understandable delicacy. The article, which is entitled 'Working-Class Attitudes', records an exchange at what, surprisingly, was the first meeting between the two men, in August 1959, or a year or two after their most notable books had appeared; it begins 'I'm glad that at last we've managed to meet.' Together they fix the composition of *The Uses of Literacy* and *Culture and Society* in the early to mid-Fifties, that doldrum of intellectual socialism, and carefully establish that neither book owed anything to the other. No sage can publicly afford to be a disciple too. The conversation labours the theme of working-class origins. 'We both came from working-class families', one of them remarks, and they compare village Wales and suburban Leeds. The ambiguity of the exchange lies in the situation. When a successful man speaks of the humility of his origins, he necessarily emphasises how far he has climbed, and how open the system was that enabled him to do so. The system cannot have been so oppressive, then; but if it was not, protest is so much the harder to justify. 'Most of us didn't regard ourselves as poor', one of them remarks, reporting that his father's wage was two pounds and more a week. Does that imply '. . . and we were not' or '. . . but really we were'? Both seem to sense the shadings and gradings of English social life and the inadequacy of terms like

'working class' and 'middle class' to meet the realities of British life;
but that question is too subversive of conventional socialism to be
pursued.

A similar ambiguity surrounds the relationship of most of the
sages to the Communist Party. In the case of Hill and Thompson,
the matter is clear in outline: they joined in youth, in the Thirties or
early in the Second World War, and left in 1956–7 with the Soviet
invasion of Hungary. What is unclear is why that invasion mattered
so much to them: the Soviet invasions of Poland in September 1939
had been condoned or supported, after all, and of Finland and the
Baltic states soon after. The Hitler–Stalin pact of August 1939 failed
to outrage, but the restoration of a Communist dictatorship in
Hungary was enough to shatter the allegiance of a lifetime. Had the
facts changed, or had they – or had both? Hill's speech of resignation to the 1957 Easter Congress of the British Communist Party
does not clearly answer this question, and its very obscurity may be
significant. 'We have been living in a world of illusions', he told his
Party comrades. 'That is why the twentieth congress of the Soviet
Union and [the 1956 invasion of] Hungary came as such a shock.
We had not been prepared for these events by our leaders. We have
lived in a smug little world of our own invention.' That makes Hill
sound like a simple dupe, which is unlikely, and an implausibly
gullible one. Why should a Fellow of Balliol wait for his opinions to
be prepared for him by his Party leaders? But the rest of his state-
ment is in any case hardly compatible with a claim to honest ignorance: 'Some of us, including myself, have a grave responsibility
for having hushed up some of the things we knew'.[5] So he had always
known something to be wrong, and had prevented others from
knowing it. But if he knew, why did he wait?

The cases of Hoggart and Williams are more mysterious: they are
at once less well documented and harder to interpret. There is no
clear evidence that Hoggart ever had connections with official communism, and only a little that he held fashionable Popular Front
views in 1936–8 when he was studying English at Leeds. There is a
letter in the university magazine which is probably his, calling on
the Church to make of Christianity a revolutionary youth
movement:

> Far from shunning such things as politics and economics, it must
> lead the way to the new conception of its faith and doctrine em-

bracing and setting the true values on all such things. The modern situation has no use for the outworn theology of yesterday. It needs a new fiery faith, offering both spiritual and material content,

and the Church must realise that Christianity is 'a revolutionary, nay, a Communistic', faith.[6] It would be surprising if he remained altogether untouched by the Marxist enthusiasm of the late Thirties. But what counted for more were the novels of D. H. Lawrence, then widely imagined to have been the chief, almost the only, representative of the proletarian spirit in English letters, and the countervailing influence of the style and elegance of his Leeds professor, Bonamy Dobrée. But the early documentation is too thin to allow for more than guessing.

The other instance is better documented. On 23 January 1940 Williams supported Will Gallacher, the Communist Member of Parliament, against a motion at the Cambridge Union which condemned the Soviet Union for 'its recent unprovoked attack upon Finland', with Gallacher insisting that all things were justified in the Soviet cause:

> It was a principle of international law that small states unable to defend themselves or to preserve their neutrality might be invaded. The Soviet Union was opening up a great vista of a brave new world, which could, however, only come into being – as could all revolutionary changes – with the accompaniment of pain and labour.[7]

Shortly after, on 27 February, the Union held a debate on the freedom of the press, in which Williams complained that all British newspapers except the *Daily Worker* expressed the same view, and attacked the capitalistic control of the press. He 'proved himself to be the most convincing exponent of Communist doctrines at present among the members of the House, and his speech had at least the merit of sincerity',[8] as the report ran. On 12 March, the day Finland announced her surrender to the Soviet Union and the cession of one-tenth of her territory, a 'Hands Off Russia' banner was raised in the Cambridge Union, and the chamber carried a motion 'That this house views with disapproval the sending of any military aid to Finland.'

It is equally clear, however, that by the end of the war, or soon after, Williams had abandoned his Communist allegiance. His shortlived periodicals *The Critic* (1947) and *Politics and Letters* (1947–8), which ran only to a few numbers before collapsing for lack of funds, were strenuously Leavisite in an old Cambridge–English tradition, but decidedly un-Stalinist in their politics, and even offered the hospitality of their columns to George Orwell. *Scrutiny* and the cult of T. S. Eliot seems to have pushed Moscow out, in his last year or two as a Cambridge undergraduate. *Culture and Society* was written in the early to mid-Fifties, its Conclusion being penned during the Suez–Hungary crisis of October 1956; and it represents a barely hopeful attempt to recover out of an English tradition of radical literature between Cobbett and the Fabians a native faith worthy to supplant a corrupted Stalinism. It is a very socialist book, and in some ways a Marxist one, but plainly not a Party manifesto. 'The only thing that matters', he wrote a few years later, 'is the reality of Socialism', calling for a revival of Marxism based on 'a recovery of something like its whole tradition'. Even so, a youthful enthusiasm for Stalinism still looked worth justifying, though in oblique and apologetic terms. In the Thirties, he wrote in 1961,

> Fascism had little to offer but terror . . . Soviet Communism, on the other hand, not only carried through an industrial revolution necessary in a backward country, but, much more crucially, carried through a cultural revolution which is not only an absolute human gain but which seems, still, in its achievements and its weaknesses alike, a specific product of a particular system. [9]

This is nearly identical in substance, though not in style, with the official Soviet position about the Stalinist years which has prevailed since Krushchev's speech to the xx th Party congress in 1956. It does not in itself provide much evidence of any departure from the Party line. The Soviet example was still to be admired with reservations, as late as 1961, and still to be blessed: 'It is difficult in the end to argue that the kind of society being created there is a negation of what is usually understood as the Marxist ideal.' This is a tightrope-walk of an argument, and the balance is perilous. Marx was wrong, Williams goes on to concede, in his prediction that industrial states would pass through capitalism to socialism, since socialist revolutions have in the event mainly occurred in backward and rural societies; that is not 'the way the world is going'. But what Marxism has to say about imperialism 'seems to me to make better sense than any other version of this now commanding issue', and peasant revolutions in China and Cuba are to be justified as 'an organic development of Marxism rather than a mere contradiction or abandonment of Marx'. So Marx was right if his assertions are reinterpreted in a Pickwickian sense. Often, in reading the sages of the New Left, one is reminded of the theological ingenuities of Christian modernism: not 'Honest to God', now, but 'Honest to Marx'.

The proximity of all this to the official Party line, first Soviet and later Chinese, often passes unnoticed; and even when it is noticed it is often understated. A double assumption is too easily accepted about the New Left: that it was not a Communist movement, and that it was not so much Marxist as *marxisant*. These assumptions may be true of many of its disciples; but they are not plainly true of its leaders. Of course, if 'Communist' means of the Party, then it is easy to show that the New Left was independent of the Party, and that it was even at times a thorn in its flesh. It is not clear, however, that this is a sufficient reason for denying its essential orthodoxy. On Soviet home policy, apart from the treatment of dissidents, on Soviet foreign policy before 1956, and on ideological questions generally, there have been few enough disagreements. The New Left never demanded an end to the one-party state in Russia. The monolithic political system created by Lenin after October 1917 was never brought into question by its debates in the Sixties, and the name of Lenin himself in those days stood beyond all possibility of criticism. The *May Day Manifesto* of 1967–8 backs Soviet foreign policy before Budapest to the hilt. During the Cold War, it argued,

> Russia was portrayed [by the West] as an aggressive imperialist power, subverting western states by promoting revolutionary activities within their borders, while threatening them militarily with the might of a fully mobilized and victorious Red Army. . . . This account had never been true, even from the beginning. For the popular resistance movements in occupied Europe during the Second World War can be seen as agencies of Soviet imperialism only by the most grotesque historical distortion. They constituted authentic popular movements, with authentic revolutionary aspirations. . . . Far from giving overt and covert support to these movements in the immediate post-war period, Stalin was careful to withhold support from all revolutionary movements in western

or southern Europe when these might conflict with the agreements as to spheres of great-power influence entered into at Yalta.[10]

Stalin is seen as the righteously injured party, cautious even to excess; the Greek resistance received 'neither aid nor encouragement from the Soviet Union' in 1945, and Stalin only reluctantly accepted Tito's assumption of power in 1945 and Mao's in 1949. If Stalin repressed opposition in Eastern Europe, this was 'in some part a consequence of the siege mentality and political degeneration occasioned by western pressure', and the Berlin blockade was caused by American encouragement of 'Western German resurgence'.[11] This account, it is true, is followed by a brief reference to 'the idiocies and crimes of Stalin's last years',[12] but that remark cannot refer to his more massive exterminations, since these occurred in the Thirties and Forties. Indeed Williams is on record elsewhere as not always or consistently opposed to that. 'I remember feeling, in the late 1930s', he wrote in 1961, 'when political terror was being used both in the Soviet Union and in Nazi Germany, how much strength there seemed to be in the argument that these were really the same kinds of society: the new kind of totalitarian state. But I eventually rejected this conclusion then, and I reject it now.' This was on the ground already quoted: that, unlike fascism, Soviet communism had 'not only carried through the industrial revolution necessary in a backward country' but a cultural revolution too.[13] This suggests that mass terror and extermination can be justified, in this system of belief, provided that the industrial and cultural rewards are sufficiently high. It also confirms that ignorance of the Terror was not a condition of intellectual Stalinism in the Thirties.

There is no grave difficulty in identifying this position. It is a sort of latter-day Stalinism with a gloss of cultural analysis. Even the word 'democratic' is used in a classic Party sense: United States aid to Greece, according to the *May Day Manifesto*, 'had served to bolster a series of corrupt and anti-democratic régimes' between 1946 and 1958. So Greece, in this use of language, was not a democracy in the 1950s. The purity of these doctrines, in the chemical sense of the word, cannot seriously be doubted. This was once the Soviet line and by the 1960s had become, most characteristically, the Peking line.

It is not usually noticed, moreover, that the heroes of the New Left were commonly members of a Communist Party. Lenin must stand first in line: he was the god of the New Left, and it would be hard to find any fundamental disparagement of his life or works in any document of the school before Solzhenitsyn's *Gulag Archipelago* began to appear in the West in 1974. More Party men follow in the canon of New Left saints: Mao Tse-tung; Ho Chi Minh, whose first syllable, shouted thrice, became the slogan of street demonstration; Che Guevara; Angela Davis, a member of the American Communist Party; Jimmy Reid of Clydeside, a member of the British; and Pablo Neruda of the Chilean, eventually Allende's ambassador in Paris. Set these names together, and the alleged independence of the New Left from the Party becomes hard to sustain and essential to qualify. In the fragmentation of official communism that occurred after the Hungarian invasion and the Sino-Soviet split of the early 1960s, the New Left looks much like an intellectual fragment representing the Peking view in a nation where official communism is almost entirely pro-Soviet.

What is more, the New Left always believed in old-style socialism at home. In its domestic policies it was New only in the sense of being a revival of the Old. Its relations with the Labour Party showed it to be strenuously anti-revisionist, fiercely loyal to Clause Four and fearful of any attempt to reinterpret socialism by any greater tolerance for the principles of market economics or any questioning of nineteenth-century orthodoxies like the class war. Anyone who suggested that modern capitalism was ceasing to be 'class-structured' could always depend on a rap on the knuckles from the New Left. In domestic affairs it was diehard socialist. 'Our task is urgent', wrote Norman Birnbaum in the foreword to *Out of Apathy*. 'Influential sections of the Labour movement have proposed the abandonment of further experiments with common ownership – and therewith, the abandonment of socialism – just when the successes of the Soviet Union foreshadow large political gains for the Communist parties in western Europe.' Gaitskellism, it was resolved, shall not pass.

In its canon of heroes, then, and in much of its policy, the New Left was strenuously anti-revisionist. But this leads into a puzzle. For in one respect, at least, it always claimed to be revisionist. It totally backed Destalinisation in the Soviet Union; *Out of Apathy* complained that not enough had yet been done in that direction. The Williams article of 1961 condemns extermination as a political weapon, though only in retrospect, and fully accepts that it was an essential aspect of Stalin's Russia. The *New Left Review* in 1974 sympathetically reviewed the first volume of *The Gulag Archipelago* in an article of genuine humanity. The New Left was both for and against political violence. But that is not necessarily a contradiction: it may, after all, imply some important moral discriminations. The question needs to be enlarged upon.

Perhaps the best approach would be to list those acts of socialist violence which the New Left approved in its heyday in the Sixties; those it failed to condemn; and those which it unreservedly condemned.

Socialist violence openly approved included the overthrow of the Russian Provisional Government in October 1917, the ensuing civil war, and Lenin's extermination of his enemies; the occupation of Eastern Europe by the Red Army in 1944–5 and the destruction of anti-Communist elements there; Hanoi's 'war of liberation' to annex South Vietnam in the 1960s;[14] and a wide variety of guerrilla actions scattered around around the world, including Guevara's campaign in Bolivia, the Provisional I.R.A. (with growing reservations), and the Palestinian struggle. (The last two were only dubiously socialist, it is true; but many thought them to be so.)

Violence not condemned, even in retrospect, includes the Soviet occupation of eastern Poland in 1939 and later of parts of Finland and all the Baltic states; the Chinese conquest of Tibet in 1951; and the enormous if ill-documented exterminations conducted by the Chinese Communists after achieving power in 1949, which are estimated to have totalled tens of millions.

Acts of socialist violence which were condemned make a shorter list. There are perhaps only three: Stalin's exterminations in the Thirties and after; the Soviet invasion of Hungary in 1956; and of Czechoslovakia in 1968.

Why were these last three events excluded from the approval of the New Left? The answer is not clearly offered in any New Left document; and so I propose some possible solutions in a tentative vein:

1. All three acts – Stalin's exterminations, Budapest and Prague – were committed by the Soviet state. If the New Left was essentially a Maoist fragment in rebellion against a pro-Soviet British Communist Party, then these positions look self-consistent and even natural.

2. All three acts were committed against other socialists. This proposition is only doubtfully true, but it was fully accepted by the New Left. Stalin's purge of the late Thirties was of Old Bolsheviks, among others, and a loyal Leninist might indeed have cause to resent it. And it was readily assumed, and often proclaimed, that the Hungarians and Czechs were seeking their own 'roads to socialism'. Nobody, on the other hand, imagined that the Tibetans were socialists in 1951.

3. All three were acts committed by the obviously strong against the obviously weak. If it is right to suppose that the youthful idealism of the New Left was not merely rhetorical, then an instinctive reaction of horror as the Russian tanks rolled into Prague must count for something. That reaction was common to almost the whole of British, and indeed, Western opinion in 1968: it would be surprising if the New Left were untouched by it. Their idealism was surely in some sense real, if selective: it was for Chinese invasions and against Soviet invasions.

★

Behind the headlines and the street demonstrations, the New Left was always and emphatically a movement of lofty intellectual pretension. Its language was laboriously polysyllabic, its obsessions intensely abstracted. This was a world of dizzying extremes. A vast, schizophrenic gap separated its two hemispheres: one a sort of political equivalent of soccer hooliganism, disrupting universities or shouting 'Ho, Ho, Ho Chi Minh' to a line of policemen in a swaying mob; the other the earnest and subdued atmosphere of the *groupuscule*, solemnly debating in a bedsitter the sociology of thought or the theory of 'structures of feeling' in companionable or fissiparous coteries. That life was no more schizophrenic, it may be argued, than the life of an Eton schoolboy who divides his day between mathematics (or Greek verse) and football. With the New Left, however, work and play were reversed. For the schoolboy, Greek is work and football is play. But in the intellectual progress of Marxism since the war, it is ideas that are toys, albeit in the most solemn of games; it is in physical action like a demo or guerrilla violence that reality ultimately exists. Ideas are what keep you happy, more or less, while the world waits for revolution. Sartre, even in his existentialist days, always insisted that the ultimate truth lay in revolution, the propositions of philosophy being worthy of attention only as intellectual diversions while one stood in wait. The metaphysic of the New Left, in a similar way, was a plaything to keep the faithful occupied. That is why it would be mistaken to regard the decline of intellectual Marxism in the 1970s as a lasting fact, just as it is now obvious that it was mistaken to have taken its decline in the 1950s as likely to last. It can re-emerge when the world situation encourages it to do so. And its ideal conditions for emergence would· be similar to those of the Vietnam war, when an international Communist interest could be made to coincide with a popular campaign at home.

Some of these metaphysical toys, however, deserve a brief dissection.

The sages of the New Left were deeply committed to an analysis of contemporary culture. On the most immediate and practical level, this amounted to a preoccupation with the mass media, as in Hoggart's part in the Pilkington Report or Williams's study *Communications* (1962). Hoggart's collection of essays, *Speaking to Each Other* (1970), sums up this preoccupation in its very title, though he belongs to the mildest, most pragmatic and most literary extreme of the movement. His views are marked by a distaste for private ownership and advertising and a veneration for state monopoly which the socialist mind traditionally, if inexplicably, associates with liberation. The state, in this view, though already by far the biggest capitalist, should be bigger still; and though the B.B.C. already predominates in broadcasting, it ought to dominate altogether. It was always one of the curiosities of this revolutionary movement that it thought big capital should be bigger, provided only it belongs to the state, and cultural power concentrated even more efficiently than it already is.

The preoccupation with culture was itself intensely historical. A Victorian emphasis is altogether intelligible, since socialism is a Victorian doctrine: it amounted to a return, and often a nostalgic one, to the roots of ideology in an age when its scriptures were first composed and when history itself seemed about to fulfil the Marxist prediction of class war in the new industrial states. Some of its jargon is readily identifiable: 'social', in the historical prose of the New Left sages, as in R. H. Tawney's before them, commonly means almost nothing at all: it is a term of art that can be removed from many a sentence without loss of sense; but then if you believe that all reality is social, or have once believed it, that is only to be expected. (The word 'societal' was soon adopted to fill the gap left by the devaluation of 'social' itself.) 'Central', too, is a key word in such prose: its origins lie in the *Scrutiny* of the 1930s and 1940s, where it became a cult word to applaud a familiar Cambridge species of moral edification through literary education; in New Left prose it continued to mean 'on our side', so that the writings of Carlyle, Ruskin and Morris might be called central in a way that Tennyson's and Meredith's were not. A minute stylistic critique of New Left prose in the Sixties would be largely unrewarding: it was bad prose, fat with syntactical excess and reverent of obscurity. But it was a prose in the last degree academic, and its badness was always cap-and-gowned: not merely polysyllabic, but laborious in syntax and intensely abstract in terminology. Much of it looked as if it had been recently and imperfectly translated from a German academic treatise of the nineteenth century. Perhaps its most extravagant instances relate to the criticism of films, in that context invariably called 'film'. Even the liveliest of twentieth-century popular arts could be reduced through the rhetoric of the New Left to the obscurity of a German forest.[15]

The cultural analysis of the Victorians, being based on an exclusive reading of favoured texts, flourished in a heady indifference to historical research. This is the richest area of fantasy in the mythology of the New Left, and facts of history were rarely allowed to violate it. The British industrial revolution of the nineteenth century was unremittingly seen as an age of triumphant *laissez-faire*, in spite of the Factory Acts; an heroic working class was invented to oppose a capitalism red in tooth and claw; and a band of courageous thinkers and writers were glorified for speaking the truth in defiance of a parliament representing only the hypocrisy of a possessing class that seldom heeded the cry of hunger. The New Left sage, rightly enough, saw himself as the natural successor to the Victorian social critics. He was above all a moralist, like them, and his concern for exact historical realities was no greater than Carlyle's or Ruskin's.

Some of the master myths of the New Left were vividly at odds with one another, and its own sense of mounting epistemological confusion began to weaken its confident cohesion even before the Sixties were out. Social conditioning was among the most agonising. Marx had held that mankind is subject to the conditioning of social circumstance, but equally that (as he put it in the *Third Thesis on*

Feuerbach), 'circumstances are changed precisely by men'. In his modern disciples, this conflict grew none the easier through debate. Man is a master; but he is also a slave. He can choose to be or have anything (*'Soyez réaliste: demandez l'impossible'*); but he is also the vic‑ tim of social pressure. Subjected to his conditioning, he yet retains the power to rise above it. So his subjection cannot have been total. But where, if it is not total, does it begin and end?

The sociology of thought cultivated by the New Left was always a massively reductive system, and in the end it was to sink under the weight of its own increasing subjectivism. Its struggle for survival paradoxically depended on excluding itself from its own system. Conditioning, like 'structures of feeling', is essentially what other people are supposed to have. Just as few socialists imagine that the doctrine of equality applies to themselves, so none supposes that his own political convictions are the result of social pressures similar to those he claims to observe working upon others. There can be few, if any, Marxist intellectuals who suppose themselves to be Marxists because social conditioning made them so. Every individual, surely, to the extent that his belief is serious, believes that he thinks as he does because what he thinks is true. That, in principle, is an entirely acceptable assumption. But what are we to say to the man who tells us, in effect: 'I am a Marxist because Marxism is true; but you are a liberal, because nurtured in a parliamentary state like the British. . .'.

Sometimes the answer to this sort of thing is clear and simple. It happens that my own upbringing was in the Thirties, in an atmos‑ phere more or less Popular Front. So it cannot be true that I believe as I do because of conditioning, if 'conditioning' means early intellec‑ tual influence. If it includes the total social and economic system as well, then the case, as matter of ordinary observation, is still weak: most young Poles, Czechs and Yugoslavs, when free to talk, express an indifference to Marxism that often borders on contempt or hatred. On grounds of observation, the sociology of thought pursued by the New Left always looked implausible. Anyone can reasonably claim exemption from it, even those who affect to believe it. And to claim that exemption is the only reasonable course: it is a liberty one might well be proud to claim and to avow.

It was an attendant assumption that the truth of a proposition is weakened or destroyed by demonstrating, or claiming to demonstrate, that it was based on social conditioning. This is a sur‑

prising assumption. Suppose, to put the matter at its simplest, that I believe X for no reason but that I was brought up to believe it. This is doubtless a highly inadequate reason for believing it. But it is also a highly inadequate reason for rejecting it. The truth-content of X remains whatever it is. Even if one only prefers the parliamentary system to one-party socialism because of upbringing, the case for parliamentarism is neither the better nor the worse for that – like the case for supposing that two plus two equals four. The truth of a proposition is independent of the factors that cause it to be believed or disbelieved.

★

The New Left was widely accepted from the start as a youth move-ment. In its leadership, at least, it was never that. At the climax of its shortlived success, in 1968–9, its literary leaders in Britain were aged between their mid-forties and their mid-fifties. They were already everything implied by the word middle-aged. One may wonder if, in intellectual history, there ever was such a thing as a youth move-ment. The young copy: they do not invent. The Children's Crusade was not devised by children. In Hitler Youth rallies, middle-aged men with bare knees marched in front. And in universities in the Six-ties the protest movement was not merely captured by such men: it was their intellectual creation from the start. They wrote the books and articles, gave the lectures and edited the journals, and demonstrated in Grosvenor Square. More than one former student militant has since revealed that he knew nothing of organised protest until he reached a university and heard it in a lecture. Enthusiasm, once kindled, might pass from student to student; but it was not in-vented by a student. Even the leadership of our political parties was a contributory influence here. Many wondered when, in the late Six-ties, the shy, demure student of earlier years turned into a jargon-stuffed oaf screaming. abuse and obscenities. But in 1963–5 two political parties elected middle-aged leaders publicly praised for a virtue called 'abrasiveness'. Some of our parliamentary life, before the New Left was born, had already turned into a public model that was harsh and crude.

The middle-aged men who made and led the New Left, however, were often content to leave abrasiveness to their disciples. In Britain, at least, the sage at his most characteristic was bland. His literary tone was as far from the revolutionary as the artifices of style could render it. Edward Thompson, in a review of Williams's *Long Revolution*, wittily imagined the book to have been written by 'an elderly gentlewoman and near relative of Mr [T. S.] Eliot, so distinguished as to have become an institution: The Tradition. There she sits, with that white starched affair on her head, knitting definitions . . . – and in her presence how one must watch one's LANGUAGE!',[16] and he appositely quoted Orwell on the revolutionary: 'Not merely while but by fighting the bourgeoisie, he becomes a bourgeois himself.' But then the sage, almost by definition, was always righteous in his own eyes; and to be left-wing, or once to have been that, necessarily and always guaranteed virtue. Left may be mistaken, in its own view; but Left is never bad. 'I have been encountering the paradox', wrote Thompson in 1973, reproving a backslider who had escaped from Eastern Europe, 'that many of those whom "reality" has proved to be wrong still seem to me to have been better people than those who were, with a facile and conformist realism, right.'[17] That enviable conviction would indeed justify all, and a claim to an especial and superior virtue rings consistently through the annals of the Old Left and the New.

Since the death of D. H. Lawrence in 1930, these were almost the first literary intellectuals in England to seek to embody the fading myth of a revolutionary proletariat. Like Lawrence in his later years, they consistently exaggerated the humility of their origins, or allowed them to be exaggerated. Their parentage was sometimes humble, but rarely of the humblest; their education was always better than average, and often much better; and they all entered universities and prospered there, years before the Butler Education Act of 1944. They later attained rank and affluence. Their self-pity ought not to be easily indulged. Early in *The Uses of Literacy* Hoggart, in answer to his question 'Who Are the Working Classes?', estimates the normal weekly wage of those he describes at 1954 prices; and though I have never thought of myself as working class, I can well remember living on less than half that figure for years. The myth of deprivation here is a highly implausible myth. Many millions of their compatriots in the Thirties and Forties were poorer than these men.

In the political struggle of the Sixties, especially inside universities, the sage took up a vantage-point of tactical interest. It is a position hard to define: perhaps it might best be called the Extreme Right of the Extreme Left. The middle-aged academic, watching his fading

Marxist convictions almost miraculously revived by an unexpected turn of history, suddenly found himself no longer a mere survivor of the Thirties but a possible centre of attention. Who in the Fifties could have guessed that the young of the Sixties, eager for a sense of community, would think they had found it in Victorian socialism or a vanishing subculture of our industrial life? Pastoralism was stronger than we had dreamt.

But the situation must have had its unnerving aspects. The new acolytes were a surprising species: they were not the children of the Jarrow hunger marchers but of prosperous parents. Sir Geoffrey Jackson has remarked of his imprisonment by Tupamaro guerrillas in Uruguay that his kidnappers all seemed to him upper-middle-class, or his social superiors in origin. The sage was hardly a prisoner like the ambassador, and his emotions must have been, for the most part, more consoling: a sudden joy at finding himself taken seriously by the young; a gush of pride at being accepted by those who were themselves socially so acceptable; and a sudden discovery that a social origin once felt to be uninteresting if not positively embarrassing might, in a new atmosphere, be turned to an undreamt-of account. Such sages are as remote as imagination can conceive from the hairy revolutionaries they contrived for a time to lead. They were prosperous, and wished to be more so; they were at least as anxious for academic promotion as most of their colleagues, and commonly attained it; they found it more than acceptable, in reviewing the books of other men, to drop the titles of their own in casual references; their life-style was more than moderately comfortable. Not less than most they loved silver on the table, a big car and Mediterranean holidays. 'It is one of the consolations of middle-aged reformers', as Saki once remarked 'that the good they inculcate must live after them if it is to live at all.' Above all, they were infatuated with the manners of upper-class life. 'I remember', wrote Hoggart of his old professor at Leeds, 'being struck right away by his "style" ' – his military phrases, his tweeds and pipe-tobacco, and his mannered voice; and he tells how the professor became a 'substitute father' for him, teaching him how to employ an 'upper-class intellectual's directness' and to drink gin.[18] All this bespeaks what might be called the soft eiderdown of English life: its eagerness to accept rebels and to absorb them, its lack of barriers, though never of distinctions, and its notorious capacity to transform the potential revolutionary into a pillar of the Establishment. The New Left sage

was an Establishment Revolutionary. A pillar was what he wanted
to become, and in Britain at least he usually succeeded.

But the ambiguity of his situation remained: that he continued to
claim and to exercise a right to condemn the system that rewarded
him handsomely and provided him with the free press and broadcasting system through which to condemn it.If the press is capitalist-
controlled, why did it print him? Because, no doubt, our press
barons are all eiderdowns too, and know what to do with intellectual
revolutionaries. The sage, in short, held revolutionary views, or at
least enjoyed the reputation of holding them, without performing
any revolutionary function. It was in that sense that he stood on the
Right of the Left. It was a tactical position, and adroitly chosen. Not
for him the pathetic fate of the ageing Theodor Adorno of Frankfurt,
complaining at a time of student violence in 1968 that he had intend-
ed in his lectures and writings only to devise a theoretical
methodology: 'How was I to know that people would try to realise it
with Molotov cocktails?' In British universities there were no
Molotov cocktails, and violence remained largely a threat.

The sage was a calculating intelligence, after all, and his
calculations were not naïve. He could attend a demonstration partly
in order to be seen, and partly to ensure that few or no windows were
broken. He might sit on a militant committee, but in order to per-
suade it not to burn down the faculty building because a consultative
committee was about to be set up, or because it had already been set
up but had not yet reported. He would insist on courses and
programmes on communications, film, Victorian social criticism
and the theory of revolution without being actively in favour of
classes or programmes of a contrary vein being broken up; but if
they were broken up, he would be against punishing the wreckers,
on grounds that would inevitably include the word victimisation.

It was a position that called for agility; but it proved, in the short
run, indispensable. In any compromise arising out of crisis, the sage
had to be there. His claim to speak for the young might not be totally
accepted, but he clearly spoke for some of them, and those the most
dangerous. On the other hand, he spoke to them as well as for them,
and could be counted on to dissuade them from the extremest
courses. He was not an arsonist, or a murderer, or even an assailant,
though infinitely understanding of the motives of those who were. In
all these ways, at least, the New Left was indeed new. It was a
system of belief rather than of action. It served international com-

munism by word and gesture, but unlike the Old Left of the Thirties it did not belong to it. It had no formal organisation, only the shifting and shiftless world of *groupuscules* sensitive to political unorthodoxy and suspicious of leaders. It had no promised land, as the Old Left had the Russia that Lenin and Stalin made. Its violence, though at times alarming, was self-expressive and served no purpose visible to the politically informed.

This was the uneasy kingdom of middle-aged men of letters whose real taste was for leisured talk and a quiet life. The world may mock the pretensions of those who, having supported in youth the greatest act of mass murder in European history, could offer themselves in maturity as the moral exemplars of a whole generation. But no man, unless the most envious, need begrudge them the fortunes they made or the enjoyment they won.

2 | *George Orwell*

An acquaintance with George Orwell goes by familiar stages. Everyone knows his two novels on totalitarian utopias, *Animal Farm* (1945) and *Nineteen Eighty-Four* (1949); many know his reports on the Depression and the Spanish Civil War; some even read his early novels. It is less widely known that he was the great English political journalist of the years surrounding the Second World War, and that for about a quarter of a century he was first and last a working journalist. But nearly twenty years after his death in January 1950, all his journalism judged to be worth keeping was brought together and edited,[1] and the accolade now seems inescapable. This is the fine flower of the literary–political consciousness of England in the mid-century. The fulfilled ambition of his short life, as he put it himself, was 'to make political writing into an art' (I, 6).* If he had only lived longer, he might have made his stature as a polemicist easier for his contemporaries to guess at; as it was, he managed only two collections of his essays before he died, and left to others to build his monument.

Journalism is the window-pane of literature, to borrow a metaphor of Orwell's own: an art, beyond any doubt, but one that leaves the writer defenceless before his public and seemingly without secrets. Never exactly a master of fiction, Orwell accepted self-exposure from the start and without demur. Even the novels are primarily self-revelations. At its most pungent, his was never a language for the delicate, or for those who can embrace only the subtler arts of suggestion. Orwell is a master of economy, but not of restraint. He loves the knock-out blow, and much of what he writes,

---

*References within brackets in this chapter relate to the original (1968) edition of Orwell's journalistic writings, specified in Note 1, p. 174 below.

at its most memorable, is the plainest diatribe. Since most men love a good diatribe, this is enough in itself to guarantee the perpetuity of his name, and I do not think it the worst reason for admiring him. There is something heroic about the spectacle: often, in his prose, one imagines him shaking off the proffered help of allies whose motives he suspects and deciding to walk alone. When Orwell called the Left Establishment of his day a set of 'Bolshevik commissars, half gangster, half gramophone, escaped quakers, vegetarian cranks and back-room Labour Party crawlers', he was writing the language of a man who felt he had enough friends in the world already, and perhaps too many; he was signing a public resignation from the official British Left and its fat connections. But his persuasive power depends on the fact that, though he openly resigned from the Left that everybody knew and knows, he never abandoned another of his own imagination. 'I belong to the Left and must work inside it', he wrote in a private letter to the Duchess of Atholl in 1945 (IV, 30), the year of *Animal Farm.* His lifelong duty, as he conceived it, was 'to attack the Right, but not to flatter the Left' (II, 323). That is understating it. It is hard, in any case, to imagine him flattering anyone.

Nobody ever understood better than Orwell how sensitive, and how vulnerable, the established Left must always be to criticism from within itself. From the Right it accepts, even welcomes, every stricture. It can soak itself in a warm bath of self-congratulation; it exists, after all, to be distrusted and feared by its enemies, and would be lost without hatred. But once attack it from within, and from the depths of its own preconceptions about human liberty and the struggle against poverty and oppression, and it can easily turn into something angry, demoralised and bitter. The Left rejects anyone who tries to switch off its halo. Being itself a criticism, it cannot think itself susceptible to criticism. It basks in a sense of immunity. Tyranny, stupidity, blindness of judgement: these are what others commit. At the most, the established Left commits mistakes. For many who belong to it, it is a bland philosophy: one of easy consolation and scarcely oblique self-praise.

What Orwell saw during the Spanish Civil War, on leave from the front in the Barcelona of 1937, was to give his mastery of deflationary rhetoric its opportunity. The Spanish Communists and their Russian allies, as he told the world in *Homage to Catalonia* (1938), were bent not on making a social revolution happen, as most

Western intellectuals believed, but on preventing one from happening. The Communists were the true conservatives: not less so because they used a well-polished rhetoric of radicalism to bamboozle the Spanish people and the world. They were cool professionals, men who had studied how to take power and how to keep it, and their professional skills extended to the use of words. But if communism is not left-wing, as he came to believe, then what is? The dizzying plunge that Orwell's mind took at this point of his life, in the late 1930s, is the theme of his finest journalism and of the two great utopias of his last years, and it will take more time than the political consciousness of Europe has yet had to absorb its full significance. What if the spectrum of Left, Centre and Right should itself prove an illusion?

The thought is unsteadying, but it must be faced. Europeans inherit these terms from revolutionary France and the politics of certain Continental states in the nineteenth century; they were hardly current in British politics before the 1920s. By Orwell's time they seemed to have achieved a convenient finality, and when you used them you thought you knew where you were. Socialism, headed by the Russian experiment after 1917, was on the Left; fascism, after the rise of the dictators, was supposed to be on the Right. The parliamentary parties of France and Britain were broadly scattered between the two poles. This is the model of political conviction that even the most reflective of men took for granted. And it makes for a good game: the rules are well known, and anyone can play. The trouble is, as Orwell came to see, that little or none of it is true.

By the beginning of the war Orwell was already clear in his mind that the spectrum of Left and Right was something worse than a crude simplification. It was an illusion: an illusion, what is more, carefully promoted by dictatorships interested in the easy conquest of the intellectual mind. On what grounds, for instance, is fascism to be regarded as right-wing? What good reason is there, he asked in an essay of 1940, for doubting that Hitler is a kind of socialist? After all, he called himself one, and we have only the word of his enemies that he does not mean what he says. 'The propertied classes', he wrote then, 'wanted to believe that Hitler would protect them against Bolshevism, and ... the Socialists hated having to admit that the man who slaughtered their comrades was a Socialist himself. Hence, on both sides, the frantic efforts to explain away the more and more striking resemblance between the German and the

Russian régimes.' And then history conveniently delivered its own demonstration: 'Then', as Orwell put it, 'came the eye-opener of the Hitler–Stalin pact' of August 1939. And yet, to consider the doctrine of the class war as coolly and as gravely as it deserves, any socialist state will have to destroy its bourgeoisie; and since that class is numbered by the millions, extermination is inseparable from its fulfilment. 'National Socialism *is* a form of Socialism,' he wrote, taking courage in both hands, '*is* emphatically revolutionary' (ii, 25).

The argument is arresting, but not as arresting as the conclusions Orwell proceeded to draw from it. There are great walls of silence, as he noticed, around the central assumptions that unite the official Right and official Left: areas that each of the two opponents suspiciously neglects, since each urgently needs the other to justify his own existence. Right and Left are equally expert at shadow-boxing. 'You don't want Jones back,' as the pigs tell the other animals in *Animal Farm* when things go badly, hinting darkly at counter-revolution. The trick is played by both sides in the political duel, and it is the trick of pretending only two possibilities exist. But when man asserts the freedom to ask why the choices are limited to two, neither Left nor Right has a sufficient answer. Each, for example, is buoyed up by an easy assurance of class support: the poor, it is officially assumed, tend to be Left, and the rich Right. But is there any real evidence for this? Both claims depend largely on simple assertion. The Right claims that the Left will expropriate private wealth; the Left, that socialism will end poverty. But leave the drawing-room and talk to people as they live their lives: is it really true that radicals, by and large, are poorer than most people? Is the assumed connection between socialism and the working class anything more than an assumption? 'I have never met a genuine working man who accepted Marxism', Orwell once told Humphry House in a letter of 1940 (i, 532). There is no fear of a dictatorship of the proletariat, he went on, but plenty to fear from 'a dictatorship of theorists, as in Russia and Germany'. The masses, meanwhile, who are ideally supposed to be dedicating their lives to ideologies like Marxist–Leninism, are in simple fact thinking about other things; the real danger is never from them, but from those who claim to speak in their name.

The long-standing enthusiasm of the official Left for economic planning and state control is another suspicious circumstance. Orwell, like many men of the Forties, believed that large increases in the economic role of the state were inevitable, no matter who might take office. But one question still remains to be put: why do socialist intellectuals *want* the state to be all-powerful? One would expect individual liberty to count more for them than anything else: more than mere efficiency, certainly (even granting that state control is usually efficient); and more, if they value liberty enough, than the abolition of poverty itself. Orwell believed that most of them were merely thoughtless; they had failed to count the cost, in human terms, of what state planning could do to the life of mind. If the artist is an autonomous individual, he once wrote, then 'the golden age of the artist was the age of capitalism. He had then escaped from the patron and had not yet been captured by the bureaucrat' (III, 229). If capitalism is doomed, then so is civilisation itself (III, 230): the dilemma may be a bitter one, for some, but it has to be faced. Socialists, he urged in *The Road to Wigan Pier* (1937), ought at least to try to understand that their ideals of efficiency and the machine-production of everything under the sun – 'a completely mechanized, immensely organized world', as he called it with distaste – might honestly repel men of sensitivity and goodwill. It is not that the socialist ideal is impractical: on the contrary, it is all too likely to happen. It is simply that we have no good reason to want it. 'I have very seldom met a convinced Socialist', he wrote, 'who could grasp that thinking people might be repelled by the *objective* towards which Socialism appears to be moving.' This is not, as both sides are given to suggesting, a simple choice between the left-wing good we would have and the right-wing reality that we face. Soviet planning is as much a reality as the Lancashire of the Depression or the life of the destitute in Paris and London. If we reject the one, we still need a better reason than has yet been given to embrace the other.

And revolution, he believed, can be no answer. Certainly the classic examples of Russia and Spain hold out no salvation – nothing, indeed, but dire warnings to those who studiously attend to the evidence. An easy progression from civil violence to dictatorship is what *Animal Farm* recounts as a process, and what *Nineteen Eighty-Four* demonstrates in its completed form. Socialism becomes state capitalism, and state capitalism is slavery. After a violent revolution, in modern conditions, there is little or no possibility of any other progression. When men believe there is a fire in the house, they do not call an incendiary: they call a fire-engine. The party of planning becomes the hero of the moment; and it will seize its chance to take control for ever and ever. Simply to talk of revolution, then, is to help the dictator in his search for power through anarchy. 'A revolution', he wrote in his diary in 1940, 'starts off with wide diffusion of the ideas of liberty, equality etc. Then comes the growth of an oligarchy which is as much interested in holding on to its privileges as any other governing class' (II, 355). Beginners make big claims for revolution, and entertain large hopes. But it is not in practice a way of changing society: it is a way of keeping it the same. New faces with a new rhetoric, indeed; but soon it is hard to tell the new rulers from the old. 'The creatures outside', runs the last sentence of *Animal Farm,* 'looked from pig to man, and from man to pig, and from pig to man again; but already it was impossible to say which was which.'

But for Orwell this is not a doctrine of despair. The future holds other possibilities than disaster. Orwell was a patriot as well as a radical, and held that the reforming way of the British can again change the world, as it has already changed it. Reform really changes. The trouble with revolution is that, by contrast, it can only conserve. It is the will-o'-the-wisp of the Left, the error that tempts it, again and again, to wander off into a void where it can easily be destroyed by its opponents. The Left has allowed itself, in this view, to be tricked into revolution by its enemies.

But then the very language of the Left, as Orwell saw with a terrible clarity, is the language of another age. Theirs is an inherited rhetoric, the liturgy of an ageing and decrepit religion; and the parlour socialist who uses terms like 'proletariat' and 'bourgeoisie', 'dialectic' and 'reification', is mouthing polysyllables from other ages and other lands. This is not a doctrine for twentieth-century Europeans, and least of all for twentieth-century Britons. Marxism is an historical relic, born of the unique conditions of the early industrial revolution and long since falsified in its chief prophecies by events themselves. If intellectuals still believe in it, it is because they are ritualists in a post-religious age. They have lost one faith and cling desperately to another. What they have failed to notice is that this century is different from all its predecessors, including the age in which Marxism was born; and the difference, for Orwell, lies in the new powers that technology has conferred upon the state. In former ages men could only dream utopias; now alas, we can have them. And the thought that men can now be forced to live the tidy patterns laid down for them by intellectuals is one to freeze the blood. The intellectual's dream of perfection is for Orwell the nightmare in which men may all soon be slaves. A work composed in the Reading-Room of the British Museum, or in a Bavarian prison, can become the black scripture of a future age. It is the tragic uniqueness of the twentieth century that everything, including unending hell, is now possible.

But if man once enters his world of designed perfection and regulation-from-above, as Orwell believed, he may paradoxically find himself not in a world of fixity but in one of constant change. This is the last and most pregnant of Orwell's warnings about the possible future of mankind. The totalitarian utopia, though inescapable for those who inhabit it, is not fixed: it is always changing, and mostly for the worse. It is in this sense that modern dictatorships already differ from the older and more familiar patterns of mere authoritarianism. In medieval Europe, or in Calvin's Geneva, the ordinary citizen could prudently accept the view of authority as a public act and know himself to be safe. Simple outward conformity ensured his security. But now, and in the future, the state itself can promote change as a device for purging its ruling hierarchy of elements that are losing in that struggle for power that every oligarchy conducts in secret. The Chinese Cultural Revolution might have seemed to Orwell, if he had lived to see it, the perfect archetype of the future he dreaded. 'The peculiarity of the totalitarian state', he proclaimed in a broadcast in 1941, 'is that though it controls thought, it does not fix it. It sets up unquestionable dogmas, and it alters them from day to day' (II, 136). No one, not even the oligarchs themselves, can henceforth be safe. The nightmare of the future is a utopia in constant flux.

What is more, totalitarianism denies to the citizen, by dint of propaganda, the right to believe that truth exists at all outside the present and momentary will of the Party. The Ministry of Truth in which the hero of *Nineteen Eighty-Four* works is a Ministry of Lies. It fabricates not only present events but events from the past as well, and the very record of history is subject to continuous revision in its files. Even more fundamentally still, it holds that there is, and can be, no truth beyond that of the moment. Truth is simply what the Party tells the people at a given moment through the mass media that it monopolises. Winston Smith's moment of liberation, early in Orwell's last book, is the moment at which he realises that things are what they are, irrespective of whether the Party says so or not.

Freedom, the hero writes in his secret diary, 'is the freedom to say that two plus two makes four. If that is granted, all else follows.' History was what it was, and the present what it is, whether men possess the wit and the courage to see that it is so or not. The ultimate myth of totalitarianism is the myth that all conviction is manipulable, that a man can only think as he does because he has been 'conditioned'. But even in 1984, Orwell dared to hope, there will be those who will secretly dare to deny this. 'The solid world exists,' reflects Orwell's hero secretively, 'its laws do not change. Stones are hard, water is wet, objects unsupported fall towards the earth's centre.' And no state monopoly of communications can make it otherwise or even, in the end, make it seem otherwise. Man, at least till he is caught and tortured into submission, can declare his own liberty – not just liberty of the gobbledygook of Marxist polysyllables, but of language itself. There is a world beyond the word. The first step towards preventing utopia from happening is to purify language to the point where it can explain things as they are.

Orwell is perhaps the supreme example in our times of the intellectual who hated intellectuals – not as individuals, that is to say, but as a caste. The case is not altogether unique. Swift, an author he admired, is another. Events since Orwell's death have not made it easier to dismiss his fears as fantasies, or his hatreds as jealousy of writers more successful than himself. He gives cogent reasons for hating and suspecting the intelligentsia he knew. Orwell saw that they did not merely accept a dictatorship of violence, but actively wanted it. The life of the mind, feeding on images of perfection, is romantically fascinated by the life of action. To write a book is all very well: but to take gun in hand – this, especially to one who has never seen war or revolution, is an ideal to titillate and compel. True, there are numerous and significant differences between Orwell's world and ours. Violent intellectuals since the Sixties have had no promised land, not even Cuba. More practically, they have no territorial base from which to work. It is even doubtful if they have a political organisation: nothing, at any rate, in terms of efficiency and cohesion, like the Communist cells in the Paris and London that Orwell knew. And, unlike the Left of his day, they distrust political success, preferring more often the heroic glamour of defeat. All this makes them less dangerous, though not less noisy. But if Orwell could see them now, twenty or thirty years on and still a few years short of his utopia, he might still feel that he had warned in vain.

3 | *Did Stalin Dupe the Intellectuals?*

Say that a rescue-party should see fit
To do us some honour, publish our diaries,
Send home the relics – how should we thank them?
The march is what we asked for; it is ended.
                    C. Day Lewis, 'Letter to W. H. Auden'

Many think of the literary Thirties as an age of dupes. It is now widely asserted or assumed that fashionable intellectual Marxism in those days was based on an honest misapprehension of what Stalin stood for. Poets and novelists in Britain, France and elsewhere, in that view, were easy victims of the Soviet propaganda machine: idealists at heart, they simply did not know that extermination had been an essential element of Soviet policy since Lenin's time; and when Stalin posed as a kindly Father of his People, he took them in. And then (to pursue the conventional view to the end) they discovered with the Molotov–Ribbentrop pact of August 1939 that Stalin was not kindly at all, and gave communism up.

The myth is manifold, and by now takes a variety of forms: that intellectuals, being skilled in self-deception, willed themselves into believing the Soviet Union a paradise; that Englishmen, at least, and especially young Englishmen who have recently been to good schools and Oxford or Cambridge, cannot knowingly have supported the extermination of millions; that if they appeared to do so, in certain isolated utterances, that is merely because they did not understand the real meaning of what they were saying; that most were fellow-travellers, in any case, rather than Party members, and less than totally committed to the cause; and that (as a last-ditch argument) nobody listens to such people anyway, politically speaking, to the creative artist all things being permitted now and forever more.

These are enviable certainties, but the documentary evidence does not support any of them. The problem of the fellow-traveller can best be cleared out of the way at once. It is an historical mis-understanding to suppose that his commitment was necessarily weaker than that of the Party member – and here I speak of commit-ment to the Party and its leadership, and not just to the ideology of Marxism. David Caute, in his study *The Fellow-Travellers* (1973), rightly dismisses what he calls in this context 'the fetish of the Party card'. In the United States that fetish was to become one of the numerous factual errors of McCarthyism in the 1950s, where it assumed the proportions of a noisy rhetorical refrain: '... card-carrying members of the Communist Party'. But the fellow-traveller need have been no less deeply committed than the member. I remember the novelist Howard Fast, shortly after his resignation from the American Communist Party with the 1956 invasion of Hungary, remarking that New York fellow-travellers often called him a traitor and cut him dead, while some Party members still telephoned to ask him how he was. The extremest fanatic may carry no card at all. But Mr Caute is a victim of his own fetish in the early pages of his book, where he names 'a certain reticence in their com-mitment' (p. 3) as among the characteristics of many fellow-travellers in the West. Reticence here cannot mean a disinclination to talk frankly and often; nobody ever accused the intelligentsia of that. A little later Caute calls the fellow-traveller's disillusionment with the West 'less radical, less total, less compromising' than that of the Party member (p. 5): he always retained, in this view, a par-tial faith in the possibility of progress under a parliamentary system. No doubt there were such people: but this cannot serve as a general description of such intellectuals in the mid- and late Thirties. Perhaps it is based on the easy assumption that, since such men returned to the parliamentary faith during and after the war, they can never really have given it up. My claim here is that they did give it up, and totally.

★

I do not believe in the myth of the Stalinist dupe. As myths go, it is surprising to the point of implausibility. After all, intellectuals are often in favour of violence. The dead hero of the New Left in the Sixties, Che Guevara, was often depicted as a man with a gun in his hand. Not all those who hung that poster on their walls, it is true, knew the gun was for use against one of the few reforming parliamentary governments in Latin America. But if they had known, how many of them would have cared? Reform, after all, is the enemy of revolution, and for many the gun confers heroism. It is an ancient Marxist precept that in politics the frivolous just talk while the serious take up arms. 'There is only one means', wrote Marx in 1848, 'of shortening, simplifying, concentrating the murderous death-pangs of the old society and the bloody birth-pangs of the new, only one means: revolutionary terror.' All that is clamorously reiterated in the works of the Master and echoed *ad tedium* in the public utterances of Lenin, Stalin, Castro and Mao. To suppose that any studious observer could have been attracted to communism as a doctrine without knowing about this is to fantasise in a void.

Still (as someone always says at this point), there is violence and violence, and all states use it sometimes, and everybody but the extreme pacifist supports some of it sometimes. . . . Yes, all that may be true. But not everybody thinks that violence is heroic. And not everybody is in favour of killing by the millions. Only hypocrisy can smudge distinctions like these: they exist and matter. To talk of the Communist or Fascist intellectual believing in violence is to use the verb 'to believe' in its intensive sense. It is not like accepting a disagreeable necessity with a decent reluctance. It is a belief proclaimed: it is almost a boast.

The issue of scale is above all vital. A spectrum in heroic violence could be usefully proposed here, and anyone but the pacifist might place himself somewhere along it. There is violence against oppressive, and especially totalitarian, authority, and many would be ashamed to condemn that; there is violence by an oppressed minority, somewhere in the middle of the spectrum; and there is violence by governments, such as Stalin's or Hitler's on a mass scale, or extermination. It is with this last, or belief in extermination, that I am here concerned.

The published evidence alone demonstrates with finality that many Western intellectuals in the age of Stalin did believe in extermination, in the sense of wanting it to happen. But the evidence needs to be sorted out.

★

Concentration camps are older than the Soviet Union. But the first extermination camps in Russian, and perhaps human, history were set up by a decree of Lenin in January 1918, three months after the October Revolution; in 1936 the process received a new and frightening impulse as Stalin's purge reached its climax. One recent study, Robert Conquest's *The Great Terror* (1968), estimates the total of such deaths in the U.S.S.R. at between 20 and 30 millions (appendix A); that estimate, which has been contested, would put Soviet exterminations at about three times the celebrated National Socialist figure of 9 millions.

The Soviet process began as early as 1918, and the general brutality of the Leninist regime was noticed and reported almost at once; what is more, the existence of extermination camps in the U.S.S.R. was reported in English books at least as early as 1931, before the literary vogue for communism had begun.

Bertrand Russell visited Russia in May–June 1920, and *The Practice and Theory of Bolshevism,* a book written by one who had come to believe communism 'necessary to the world', appeared before the year was out. It called Lenin's way 'rough and dangerous', and his government one of 'evil men'.[1] Russell is writing here about Lenin and Trotsky, not Stalin. As for their slogan 'the dictatorship of the proletariat': 'when a Russian Communist speaks of dictatorship, he means the word literally'.[2] It is 'proletariat', Russell adds, that the Communist understands Pickwickianly. Many of the Tsarist police are now employed at 'their old work' by aristocratic Bolsheviks who reminded Russell of young British public-school types; they will soon come to resemble 'our own government in India'.[3] H. G. Wells's *Russia in the Shadows,* based on a visit a few months later, was in some ways a retort to Russell, but it did not attempt to refute any of this. The Red Terror, Wells argues, was fanatical but honest: 'Apart from individual atrocities, it did on the whole kill for a reason and to an end'.[4] So he held extensive killing to be justified if for a reasonable end. Russell found Lenin a cruel man, Wells found him practical and refreshing. But they did not differ about the manifest fact of Soviet brutality itself.

In 1931 the Anti-Slavery Society in London sponsored and published a *Report on Russian Timber Camps* by Sir Alan Pim and Edward Bateson, which was extensively quoted in the same year by

Katharine, Duchess of Atholl, in *The Conscription of a People,* including photographs of Soviet camps. These revelations led to a public campaign to boycott Russian timber. The *New Statesman* (23 January 1932) dismissed the demand as anti-Communist fever: 'Our anti-Bolsheviks are once more sounding the tocsin.' Phrases like 'the produce of convict labour' (*The Times*) or 'the slave-manned forests of Russia' (*Morning Post*), so the *New Statesman* assured its readers years before the Popular Front began, are 'grotesque distortions of the truth'. *The Times,* it goes on, resents 'the success of the whole Five Year Plan', and its views are mere 'prejudice, hypocrisy and misrepresentation'.

Not even all Marxists accepted the *New Statesman* defence of the Soviet penal system. In the same year John Middleton Murry, arguing in *The Necessity of Communism* for Marx and against Lenin, indignantly quoted the report of a recent conference of prison authorities in the Soviet Union, where a Commissar of Justice repudiated 'attempts to reform class enemies' as a political error: 'Such prisoners must be used to Socialist purposes, but warders must abandon the practice of regarding them as individuals. They must be regarded collectively as an alien mass.' And Murry draws the plain conclusion. The ordinary criminal, in the Soviet system, may hope for release; but 'the man who happens to hold heretical views concerning the Russian–Marxian dogma is deliberately to be treated as a mere beast of burden, worked to death, and exterminated'.[5] In 1933 *Out of the Deep* appeared with an introduction by Hugh Walpole and a preface by Sir Bernard Pares, and included letters from inmates of Soviet Union timber camps describing their conditions there. A year later Malcolm Muggeridge, in *Winter in Moscow* (1934), thought the whole matter almost too familiar to be worth mentioning. Trotsky's *History of the Russian Revolution,* he suggests in his preface, 'blows the gaff as far as the Soviet régime is concerned, and should therefore save discerning readers the expense and weariness of an Intour'. The imbecile admirers of the U.S.S.R. are fed, it is true, with 'bogus statistics and dreary slogans', but they also see the facts for themselves: 'I treasure as a blessed memory the spectacle of them going with radiant optimism through a famished countryside; wandering in happy bands about squalid, overcrowded towns. . . .' And in 1935 George Kitchin's *Prisoner of the Ogpu* appeared, describing his experiences in a Soviet labour camp in 1928–32, with a map of the penal area and a list of thirteen camps, estimating the total number of prisoners at over half a million, with a probable annual mortality rate of 22 per cent.

The editor of the *New Statesman*, Kingsley Martin, though from different motives, already shared the view that enough was known about the Soviet system. 'No one wants to know any more "truth about Russia"', he wrote in 1932, in his preface to *Low's Russian Sketchbook*; the English market is already flooded with books about the U.S.S.R., and anyway he is on holiday. But he too does not doubt that the Soviet Union has already exterminated a political class. He visited Russia with these questions in mind:

> How far is it possible to change people's habits suddenly and by violence? Can you produce equality and abolish class feeling by wiping out the upper class and, if you can, is the price worth it?[6]

Long before the Spanish Civil War ever began, and long before the pro-Stalinist intellectual hysteria reached its climax in 1936–8, the blunter facts of the Soviet system were freely available in English books.'The entire British intelligentsia has been to Russia this summer', wrote Kingsley Martin hyperbolically in 1932.

A more monumental instance is still to come. A. J. P. Taylor, in a recent footnote of characteristic acerbity, has called Sidney and Beatrice Webb's *Soviet Communism: a New Civilisation?* (1935) 'the most preposterous book ever written about Soviet Russia'. There, one is tempted to feel, he may have forgotten Hewlett Johnson's *The Socialist Sixth of the World* (1939), which does not mention the labour camps at all. The Webbs, by contrast, offer extensive documentation on the subject. In chapter 7, entitled 'The Liquidation of the Landlord and the Capitalist', they describe in detail the practice of 'forcibly deporting kulaks and other recalcitrant peasants . . . to concentration camps or special industrial depots where they could be set to hard labour in return for a bare subsistence'. Some reforming steps have been taken, they add, but conditions are still 'inhuman', while 'there is authority for saying that the prisoners were, after 1930, no longer beaten, tortured or killed', though they do not quote an authority. A long footnote[7] quotes a work by an escaped prisoner, Vladimir Chernavin, called 'Life in Concentration Camps in the USSR', which he repeated in his book *I Speak for the Silent* (1935). The Webbs defend the Soviet secret police, without which, as they convincingly argue, there would be no Soviet state; and they praise their prisons in a section called 'The Constructive Work of the Ogpu'. Their argument is simple. It is a capital offence in the Soviet Union to work against the government, and so it should be. 'In Russia the greatest crime is that against the state.' In the second edition of their book in 1937, when the question mark was removed from the title, a new entry on 'concentration camps' was added to the index for the greater convenience of Soviet admirers. Years later, a niece of Beatrice Webb was to tell of an incident that occurred shortly after the Webbs' visit to the Soviet Union in 1932.

> I had asked the headmistress of one of our local secondary schools who had been on an extensive tour down the Ukraine to come and meet them. Over the teacups the headmistress mentioned her horror at finding her party in a station where several cattle-trucks of 'enemies of the State' had been pulled up at a siding on their way to Siberia. 'Very bad stage management,' said Aunt Bo severely. 'Ridiculous to let you see them; the English are always so sentimental.'
>
> At which the headmistress, rather shocked, said: 'But Mrs Webb, they were starving and held out their hands for food – they were in a pitiable condition.'
>
> 'I know,' the great one replied, 'but you can't make an omelette without breaking eggs.'[8]

The Webbs were in love with efficiency, but poets could agree with them. Many of the details in Stephen Spender's *Forward from Liberalism* (1937) are avowedly based on their book. Spender quotes Article 131 of the Soviet Constitution, which condemns all who 'violate public socialist property' as enemies of the people, and he comments:

> This law is the foundation-stone of political freedom. Above it, the whole structure may be repressive, but it will be possible gradually to knock away the repressive laws and establish complete political freedom.[9]

He is openly for a one-party state. Since communism is a moral system as well as a political one, 'no political party could arise in Russia which opposed the fundamental principles of communist morality. Communist democracy will protect itself from counter-revolution.'[10] Spender does not mention Stalin till a few pages from the end of *Forward from Liberalism,* and then favourably.

But he knows of the Red Terror, and supports it: 'If there had been no Red Terror, it is difficult to see what order would ever have grown out of the chaos of post-war Russia.' Lenin had substituted the Cheka for mass terror; and if chaos follows the next war, the best chance will lie the same way, in a 'ruthless force from which a new and juster order might emerge'.[11] Mistakes may have been made, Spender concedes, but in general Soviet policy is one of 'unavoidable necessity'.[12]

★

In the Thirties many literary intellectuals publicly advocated violence. They did not merely excuse it when it happened, but clamoured that it should. Brecht's *Die Massnahme*, first performed in Berlin in December 1930, tells of three comrades on a mission to China who kill a fourth who has endangered the cause. It is the Communist's duty, so the play concludes, to forget one's rights as an individual and to see the historic justice of murder:

> Who are you?
> Sink into the dirt.
> Embrace the butcher, but
> Change the world. It needs it.

And the three comrades are heroically unrepentant about their murder:

> It is fearful to kill.
> But not only others, ourselves we will kiil,
> If necessary.

Hugh MacDiarmid's 'First Hymn to Lenin', which first appeared in Lascelles Abercrombie's *New English Poems* in 1931 as 'To Lenin', makes the same brutal point. (Rashly, perhaps, I translate it unaided from the Lallans.)

> As necessary and insignificant as death
> With all its cruelties in the cosmos still
> The Cheka's horrors are in their degree,
> And will end sooner! What matters it whom we kill

> To lessen that foulest murder that deprives
> Most folk of real lives?

'*What matters it whom we kill?*' Even the Nazis showed some discrimination in that matter. But in the world of the Marxist intellectual, even to allow oneself the private luxury of choosing victims may be a false delicacy, and to concede a right of choice would be to forget 'that clear distinction between the necessary anarchy of thought and the essential dictatorship of action'.[13] When you join you do what you are told, however nasty. Revolution is not a game, as Cecil Day Lewis put it in the same anthology, in his 'Letter to a Young Revolutionary', 'with both sides keeping the rules and the winner jumping the net to shake hands with the loser; not even in England'. A revolutionary is a David against Goliath, and 'the Communist Party is therefore right in its severity towards deviations'. Besides, communism is working righteously against one of the deepest of all human instincts, the desire to possess: 'Even in Russia, where they know they'll get shot for it, people take the risk in order to transfer a shilling's worth of public property to a private hoard'.[14] So as early as 1933 Day Lewis knew that his adherence required breaking the ordinary moral rules, oppressing deviation and shooting people who commit petty theft. So much for the view that the Thirties poets were idealistic young men just down from Oxford who did not yet know what they were involved in.

> Only
> Submit to the visiting angel, the strange new healer,

as Day Lewis wrote in a poem he contributed at that time to *New Country*.[15] That angel had a sword, and it demanded submission as the price of victory. Another contributor, Charles Madge, in 'Letter to the Intelligentsia' a few pages on, a poem in praise of Lenin, makes of that sword a knife, and he throws in Siberia with a touch of relish:

> Only knife-edged nothing will devour
> The deviators; clean cut gone the voice
> Of the seceders; Siberian their choice;
> To left or right turning were expelled
> Trotsky and Kamenev, leaders who rebelled.[16]

Spender's *Trial of a Judge* (1938), a play that evidently owes much to Brecht, ends on a similar note of blood. The Communists proclaim their faith in these terms:

> We hold the secret hub of an idea
> Whose living sunlit wheel revolves in future years outside.
> As for our lives,
> When they are killed they fall like seeds
> Into the ground to bear the tenfold fruit
> Of our purpose . . .[17]

And the play ends with an heroic chorus of Red prisoners and a cry from the wife of a murdered Jew:

> . . . And the aerial vultures fly
> Over the deserts which were cities.
> Kill!! Kill! Kill! Kill!

while the Red chorus whispers

> We shall be free.
> We shall find peace.

The most curious case of all is that of André Gide who, as the world came to believe, returned from a visit to the Soviet Union in 1936 in a state of high-minded disillusion. That suggests how little his *Retour de l'URSS* is now read. Gide objected to Stalin because he was not brutal enough. Stalin was a backslider from Marxism, 'a divergence from the first ideal' of the Revolution; and out of a natural fear of Germany he had allowed a 'progressive restoration of the family, of private property, of inheritance', in order to encourage the citizen 'to feel that he has some personal possessions to defend'. And so the first impulse of the Revolution has been 'progressively deadened and lost' by compromise and concession. Gide was not against dictatorship as such, only the sort that he had seen in Russia: 'We were promised a proletarian dictatorship', he complained, and had been given a personal one. The epigraph to the *Retour* recounts in exquisitely literary French the Homeric story of Demeter: disguised as a wet-nurse, she had placed the infant Demophon naked on fiery embers, 'in apparent cruelty, though in reality moved by a great love', to turn him into a god, till the child was rescued by an indignant mother. How is it possible to read that little allegory except as a demand by Gide that the Soviet people should be returned to the flames of revolution? The child

> endures the fiery charcoal; he gathers strength from the ordeal. Something superhuman is fostered in him, strong and beyond all hope glorious,

before the revolutionary process is ignorantly interrupted. Gide seems to have visited Russia a few months too soon. In fact Stalin was already stoking that fiery furnace in 1935–6.

The intellectuals did not merely accept violence: they liked it and asked for more. And they got more. 'A tough, ruthless, wholly unscrupulous, iron-hearted youth, practising already in his relentless fashion the Communist doctrine that the end justifies the means' – that is how T. C. Worsley, in his autobiography *Flannelled Fool* (1967)[18], describes Esmond Romilly as a fourteen-year-old public-school Marxist who introduced him and others to the Communist Party; and he is describing what once attracted him. Nobody was having the wool pulled over his eyes. They venerated the Communist just because he did not cultivate delicacy or tell lies.

★

The veneration of violence remains a vexed question. George Orwell's 'Inside the Whale' (1940), still the best critical essay on the literary Thirties, offers an answer which is perhaps too simple to convince altogether. Orwell argued there that poets supported the idea of violence because, in their innocence, they did not know what violence was really like. Auden's poem 'Spain', he remarks scornfully, could only have been written 'by a person to whom murder is at most a *word*':

> Today the deliberate increase in the chances of death,
> The conscious acceptance of guilt in the necessary murder . . .

And Orwell attacks the literary Marxist with a jibe that has since become justly famous: 'So much of left-wing thought is a kind of playing with fire by people who don't even know that fire is hot.'

This is a very uncharacteristic passage: Orwell is not much given to easy excuses, least of all for his opponents. How does he know, in any case, that murder was only a word for left-wing intellectuals? One might half-suspect him of showing off here, as he sometimes does: he loves to present himself as an existential hero, the man who has been through it all himself; and he may be seeking an argumentative advantage, as an ex-policeman and ex-soldier, over the kind of writers who spent the Spanish Civil War at cocktail parties or well behind the front: 'It so happens that I have seen the bodies of numbers of murdered men – I don't mean killed in battle, I mean murdered. Therefore I have some conception of what murder means – the terror, the hatred, the howling relatives. . . .'[19] A biographer of Orwell would make sense of this assertion in terms of his time as a policeman in Burma. But it is notable that he does not offer any evidence for his claim that, when intellectuals advocate violence, they do not really know what they are saying. He may be right; but how does he know?

Probably Orwell was convinced, as an Etonian of that era might well be, that people like that do not do that sort of thing. A generation that has studied the careers of Burgess, Maclean and Philby is less likely to take this easy view. It is true we still do not know whether murder was committed, or even planned, within the circles that Orwell makes fun of. But the harsh noises that emerge, from *Die Massnahme* (1930) to *Trial of a Judge* (1938), do not make it utterly unlikely. History was calling upon man for a blood sacrifice. Until murder is done, he will feel immature.

Yes, why do we all, seeing a communist, feel small?

wrote Day Lewis in an uncollected poem of 1934, 'The Road These Times Must Take'.[20]

There fall
From him shadows of what he is building . . .
It is the future walking to meet us all.
Mark him. He is only what we are, mortal. Yet from the night
Of history, where we lie dreaming still, he is wide awake . . .
He is what your sons will be, the road these times must take.

Day Lewis's Party membership seems to have been confined to

1935–8. In his autobiography, *The Buried Day* (1960), which is an honest-looking book, he deplored his early achievements as 'a too quick crop, facile and superficial',[21] but does not deny what they were. And what they were was the most cynical form that youthful idealism can take:

> It is the logic of our times,
> No subject for immortal verse –
> That we who lived by honest dreams
> Defend the bad against the worse,

he wrote in 1940, in the autumn of his Marxist faith. Joining the side of a Marx-personified 'history', finding comradeship, marching in step – these are the publicly declared reasons why intellectuals in the Thirties revered violence. Bertrand Russell was the first, but far from the last, to notice that the team spirit of socialism and of the great British public schools might be seen as one and the same.

★

When and why did such men join and leave communism? It is plain, at least, that Marxist intellectuals cannot have abandoned it in or around 1939 because they discovered what it was, since they had always known what it was. Nor did they claim, at that time, to have been duped. Koestler, in *The Invisible Writing* (1954), tells in impressive detail how he lost his Communist faith in a Franco prison in 1937 and resigned from the Party in the following year – by virtue, apparently, of thinking about it at great length at the window of his Spanish cell. There he slowly came to see that human reality was more complicated than he had thought. In August 1939 'the Hitler–Stalin pact destroyed the last shred of the torn illusion',[22] but the illusion can never have been that Lenin and Stalin were men of peace. Deciding that everything is all more complicated than one had thought, however, is decidedly the note to strike here. The retreat from Moscow was a retreat from simplicity, from the black-and-white dogma of class war. If a general answer must be made, then this is the best general answer. In one's early middle age, often enough, the simpler solutions of youth cease to look true or sufficient.

The arrival date is somewhere in the very early Thirties or earlier.

Louis MacNeice, in his autobiography *The Strings Are False* (1965), puts his own attraction to communism at around the time of *New Signatures* (1932); so it was not caused by the advent of Hitler in January 1933. Middleton Murry declared himself 'finally and forever a Communist' early in 1932, though he belonged to the I.L.P. and not to the Communist Party; art and literature, he had resolved, could only be 'superficial and trivial' until revolution had happened.[23] The collapse of the Labour–Liberal Coalition in 1931, the Labour split, and the economic collapse that attended these events in 1930–2 – all this is more likely to have provided an impulse to intellectual communism than an event most intellectuals utterly failed to predict: the rise and consolidation of Nazi power across Europe.

The date of departure is always within the narrow limits of 1937 and 1941, and the Molotov–Ribbentrop pact of August 1939 is late in that process, and sometimes too late to count. John Lehmann, in his autobiography *The Whispering Gallery* (1955), designates the *Anschluss*, which he witnessed in Vienna in March 1938, as his day of disillusion. Day Lewis, in the last chapter of *The Buried Day*, tells how he left communism after a successful speech against fascism in the Queen's Hall in 1937: 'I did not, for some time yet, abandon my political beliefs', however; and even when he moved to Devon in August 1938 'I felt no antipathy yet for Communist theory, and not much for Communist practice'. The 'Dedicatory Stanzas to Stephen Spender', written during the phoney war of 1939–40 and prefixed to his version of Virgil's *Georgics* (1940), strike a warm valedictory note, the poet turning his back on politics in favour of pastoral joy, inward reflection and the delights of poetic craftsmanship:

> Spain was a death to us, Munich a mourning.
> No wonder then if, like the pelican,
> We have turned inward for our iron ration,
> Tapping the vein and sole reserve of passion,
> Drawing from poetry's capital what we can.

Louis MacNeice moved in the same direction at the same moment; and in a private letter of March 1940, written during the phoney war, he apologises to a friend for sounding like Auden:

One must keep making things which are *not oneself* – e.g. works of art, even personal relationships – which must be dry and not damp. . . . Because it seems high time neither to be passive to flux nor to substitute for it, Marxist-like, a mere algebra of captions.[24]

The movement from active anti-fascism after Hitler seized Prague in March 1939 may have been strengthened, too, by the realisation that a great majority of Englishmen and (worse still) an Establishment of bureaucrats and bishops had suddenly joined the side. A cosy group had ceased to be cosy. 'Yes, we shall fight, but . . .' Day Lewis's poem goes on: do not think we are in it for the same reason as the rest of you. Spender put the best face he could on defection, years later, in *World within World* (1951):

> Journalists sometimes complained in the Press that the anti-Fascist writers who had shown such zeal in 1936 and 1937 seemed perversely uninterested, now that the action against Hitlerism for which they had been clamouring was really taking place. But the fact was that the anti-Fascist battle had been lost. For it was a battle against totalitarian war, which could have made the war unnecessary.[25]

But Marxists have always believed that social improvement can only be achieved at the cost of massive violence, so that Spender's argument depends on emphasising the difference between approving one war and another. A 'battle against totalitarian war', whatever that means, might be somehow different from the war of 1939–45, but it would surely have been a war of some kind. In any case, much of the intellectual shift of view away from communism had already begun well before the outbreak of war in September 1939.

The year 1939 is surely the most important of all in focusing the gradual phenomenon of a loss of faith. In March, Prague fell to Hitler and Madrid to Franco; Catalonia had fallen weeks before; and in August, Stalin and Hitler publicly announced an alliance that privately included the partition of Poland in the following month. These were all events that Communists had loudly proclaimed could not and would not happen. They shook the plausibility, if not of Marxism itself, at least of the Communist Party. The Popular Front was dead. The confident literary rhetoric spilt in favour of the Spanish Republic in 1936–7, when its supporters passionately believed that they could not lose, must have seemed fly-blown even before the end of 1938. The Republic did lose – betrayed, as many rightly believed, from within. Orwell's *Homage to Catalonia*, which appeared early in 1938, had already shown that anti-fascism was far from the first consideration in the minds of Soviet commissars and those who worked for them in Spain. Russia was a power like other powers.

On the other hand, the literary evidence does not suggest that Marxist intellectuals ceased to be Marxist as early as 1939: only that they ceased, then or earlier, to believe in the Communist Party. Day Lewis's 'Dedicatory Stanzas' to the *Georgics* of 1940 suggest a loss of purpose but none of dogmatic faith. Auden's contribution to the symposium *I Believe,* which first appeared in New York in August 1939, is a revision of an article that had appeared there in the *Nation* of December 1938. If Auden made his revisions in the early months of 1939, when Spain and Czechoslovakia were falling, then Spender's account in *World within World* may have to be reconsidered. In 1937, as Spender wrote years later, Auden 'had offered his services in Spain as a stretcher-bearer in an ambulance unit. Yet he returned home after a very short visit of which he never spoke. But as a result of this visit he wrote . . . "Spain".'[26] But 'Spain' is about 'necessary murder', among other things. Auden, who was in Spain from January to March 1937, also wrote an enthusiastic article for the *New Statesman* (30 January 1937) called 'Impressions of Valencia', composed on the spot:

> For a revolution is really taking place, not an odd shuffle or two in cabinet appointments. In the last six months these people have been learning what it is to inherit their own country, and once a man has tasted freedom he will not lightly give it up. . . . That is why, only eight hours away at the gates of Madrid where this wish to live has no possible alternative expression than the power to kill, General Franco has already lost two professional armies and is in the process of losing a third.

Shortly after, in a review of Christopher Caudwell's *Illusion and Reality* for *New Verse* (May 1937), he welcomed it as a manifesto of literary Marxism. 'We have waited a long time for a Marxist book on the aesthetic of poetry', he began enthusiastically; and concluded that he would not criticise the book, 'firstly because I am not competent to do so, and secondly because I agree with it'. And when, two years later, he wrote and revised his 'Morality in an Age of Change' for *I Believe,* Auden concluded that different political parties should ideally be allowed to exist, but 'I cannot see how a socialist country could tolerate the existence of a Fascist party'. In some ages politics should be left to the professionals:

> But ours is not such an age. It is idle to lament that the world is becoming divided into hostile ideological camps; the division is a fact. No policy of isolation is possible. Democracy, liberty, justice, and reason are being seriously threatened and, in many parts of the world, destroyed. It is the duty of every one of us, not only to ourselves but to future generations of men, to have a clear understanding of what we mean when we use these words, and to defend what we believe to be right, if necessary, at the cost of our lives (p. 31).

That ringing partisanship was still active in December 1938. Early in 1939 the last sentence was revised, but in no way weakened: '. . . to defend what we believe to be right, perhaps even at the cost of our lives and those of others'.[27]

Spender denies Auden ever had 'a Communist phase'; he merely 'had a firmer grasp of Marxist ideology, and more capacity to put this into good verse', than many writers who were Communists. This is now an established convention of our literary history. Caute echoes it: 'Auden was not really ever a fellow-traveller';[28] but then Caute accepts the traditional view of Gide's defection – Auden had 'praised Gide for telling the truth as he saw it'. This argument is a house of cards, since Gide in 1936 was more of a Stalinist, as that term is now understood, than Stalin himself. If the legend of Auden's political detachment or semi-detachment were not so strong, it would seem natural to read more than one of his poems of the mid-Thirties as tracts for the time. Consider this from *Look, Stranger!* (1936):

> Those who in every county town
> For centuries have done you down,
> But you shall see them tumble down
> Both horse and rider.

Is it not merely over-ingenious to doubt that any reader of 1936 would read this poem, 'Brothers Who When the Sirens Roar', as a plain call for worker-revolution? That, admittedly, does not make the poet a member of any political party. But it does not leave him a neutral or detached figure either. And yet the conventional view was readily accepted by Monroe K. Spears, who saw these interests in the Thirties as only the mildest and briefest of flirtations: 'They [the poets] were, of course, ignorant of what was really going on in Russia. . . . But when they encountered Communist methods in Spain they were shocked'.[29] If Auden was shocked by what he saw in Spain in 1937, he signally failed to say so: in fact he publicly said the reverse. I believe Spears's version of these events, which is designed to make an impressive case for the post-war conservative Auden whom he admires, is comfortable rather than true. Much of it is based on Spender's *World within World* and on an Auden article written as late as 1955, in *Griffin*, where the poet himself offers a belated retrospect of his early views:

> Looking back, it seems to me that the interest in Marx taken by myself and my friends . . . was more psychological than political; we were interested in Marx in the same way that we were interested in Freud, as a technique of unmasking middle-class ideologies, not with the intention of repudiating our class, but with the hope of becoming better bourgeois.

The world of the 'hostile ideological camps' of 1938–9, where a man has a moral duty to choose one or the other, had been efficiently suppressed by 1955. But suppression is itself evidence that there was something to suppress. In his later years he would not allow poems like 'Spain' to be reprinted, unless with the printed qualification that he had come to consider such poems as 'trash which he is ashamed to have written'.[30] Any future biographer of Auden will be wise to recognise that to suppose there was no accusation worth answering here would make his suppression look merely silly. I believe Auden was an active Marxist revolutionary through most or all of the Thirties, probably from his year in Berlin in 1928–9 at least till his migration to the United States in January 1939; that many of his writings then, both in verse and prose, are manifestoes in a political cause; and that he later altered or suppressed them because he had ceased, in the course of the Second World War, to believe in that cause. This is confirmed by a letter he wrote to me in January 1971; and though that is late as evidence, its argument is too pertinent and detailed to be easily disregarded:

During the Thirties I and, I think, most of my friends, though we did not know the whole awful truth, were well aware that very unpleasant things were happening in Russia. For this reason I never joined the Party, because I was afraid I might have to defend the Soviet Union. The mistake we made was to think: 'What can one expect of the Russians? They are barbarians who have never had a Renaissance or a Reformation and have always lived under a dictatorship. Communism in the West would be different.' What we failed to realise was that any One-Party System of government, whether of Right or Left, is bound to be a tyranny.[31]

It seems altogether likely that the German Communist Party rather than the Russian was the object of his earliest enthusiasm; there is a letter written to a friend late in 1932 hopefully predicting a Communist revolution in Germany, a nation that had known both Renaissance and Reformation, and a full-scale industrial revolution as well. In 1932 it would look civilised in a way that Russia would not; its culture was itself highly politicised, especially in the Berlin that Auden knew; and, perhaps as important, it would look an apter fulfilment of Marx's prophecy that revolution would begin in the advanced industrial states. And, unlike Russia, Germany was a land he had lived in and loved.

Auden's Marxist enthusiasm was real. To suppose otherwise would be to make nonsense not only of deleted or revised poems but of his article for *I Believe,* which abounds in phrases like 'again, Marx seems to me correct . . .'. That he held certain views and lived a life incompatible with Marxism does not alter the fact that he was publicly committed. It is not uncommon, after all, for dedicated men to hold views and perform actions which are incompatible with their principal dedication. Anti-semites, it is said, sometimes have Jews as their best friends, and it is often a mistake to let men write their own intellectual histories without verifying them by the historian's recourse to documents.

The evidence, then, is that all the poets mentioned here were political activists, especially in the years 1936–8, and that they publicly urged the same duty upon others. The myth of poetic detachment will not wash.

★

Violence was a doctrine of sincerity, and the word is deliberately ambiguous here. In the first place, Marxist intellectuals in the Thirties were plainly sincere, in the sense of direct and outspoken, when they demanded the 'necessary' violence of Communist revolution. But violence was sincere in that age, and more recently still, in another sense: a sense that Lionel Trilling, to judge from his *Sincerity and Authenticity* (1972), might prefer to call 'authentic'. Violence makes a man real. Before he has committed it, he does not altogether belong among his comrades, or even exist. Just as some Christians have held a man should be ready to die for his faith, so the Marxist believes he should be ready to kill for it: then, and only then, does he become himself. The urbane world he lives in is unmasked for what it really is in its violent reaction to the deed; and he himself has made his sacrifice of blood. The political murderer cannot return; the deed is irrevocable. He must hunt or be hunted to the bitter end. There is a unique romance that belongs alone to the world of action. Douglas Hyde, writing as an ex-Communist in *I Believed* (1950), tells how at the age of sixteen he had heard from leftists of a 'bomb-shop' in Bristol, and 'felt let down and somewhat frustrated' to discover that the bombs were only books; and he admiringly learnt by heart Vanzetti's words on hearing his death sentence: 'I might have lived out my life talking at street-corners to scorning men. . . . Now we are not a failure.'

The steps to climb towards this ultimate conviction, with its climax in the years 1936–8, were largely built for British intellectuals long before the Spanish Civil War began. They were there in the early years of the century, in the writings of such Victorian survivors as Shaw and Wells. The steps can be listed in formal order.

1. *Liberalism is dead, as an historic fact*; it has given place to class war. And since Marx predicted class war, he may be right about other matters too. The future is all socialist, in this view, and even for non-Communists Marxism provides 'the intellectual framework of socialist thought'. Liberalism will die because politics 'are moving towards a clearer division between the possessing and the working classes'.[32] Those who clung to the Party after August 1939 even contrived to believe that Hitler, the new ally of the Soviets, might not be so bad; better, anyhow, than the French and British empires that were warring with him. 'I would sooner be a Jew in Berlin', wrote J. B. S. Haldane in the *New Statesman* of 30 September 1939, a few weeks after the outbreak of war, 'than a Kaffir in Johannesburg or a

negro in French Equatorial Africa. If the Czechs are treated as an inferior race, do Indians or Annamites enjoy complete equality?' Sean O'Casey, who between 1939 and 1941 as a member of the editorial board of the *Daily Worker* had publicly demanded peace with Hitler, then Stalin's ally, privately confessed himself bewildered after the German invasion of Russia. He had thought that the pact of 1939 between the two dictatorships must mean that National Socialism would move towards communism; 'I thought', he wrote disconsolately to a friend in July 1941, that 'Hitler would go Left'.

Liberalism was associated with private wealth and with empire, both unacceptable to the mythology of socialism. 'We are seeing the end of Liberal Democracy', wrote Auden in *New Era* (January 1939), and this is 'a good thing': it will be replaced by socialism or fascism. There were only two sides before August 1939, and anyone not for us is against us. This is how Kingsley Martin justified his rejection of Orwell's articles attacking the Communist role in the Spanish Republic in 1937, and it helps to explain why *Homage to Catalonia*, in the following year, was so coolly received by the *New Statesman* reviewer, V. S. Pritchett (30 April 1938): Orwell's liberal-anarchist defence of P.O.U.M. was 'wrong-headed' and 'perverse', so the reviewer wrote, given that Soviet support in Spain is indispensable, and Orwell was just 'kicking against the pricks'. Choose or be damned. . . .

2. *Communism was fashion,* and there are always those who would rather be Red than dead, in the fashionable sense of the term. That state of mind must be commoner than public admission would suggest. Some men choose politics as women choose hats. Russia, as Michael Ayrton later confessed of his adolescence in the Thirties, meant what Picasso meant in art: 'Both, we believed, were bastions of the *avant-garde,* to be accepted and supported regardless'.[33] Regardless of pretty much anything at all, for some. The admission is frank enough to be creditable.

3. *Communism will make a man of you.* It is not only, as Louis MacNeice confessed years later in *The Strings Are False,* that most have a violent streak that seeks its own justification ('I wanted to smash the aquarium'): it is more like the deliberate suppression of adolescence in an act of obedience, embracing the butcher. 'The strongest appeal of the Communist party', MacNeice wrote, 'was that it demanded sacrifice; you had to sink your ego'.[34] And the deeper it sank, the better.

4. *Communism gets things done.* While gradualists talk, Stalin is creating something. He goes the whole hog. 'Much better be ruled by Stalin', wrote G. D. H. Cole during the war, in his *Russia and the Future* (1942), 'than by a pack of half-witted and half-hearted Social-democrats.' Violence happens, but in a cause that counts, and omelettes are only made of broken eggs. Shaw harped on the point often in plays and prefaces. 'Let us see this matter in perspective', as the *New Statesman* wrote of the Moscow purges (5 September 1936): 'A social revolution is accompanied both by violence and by idealism. Its success must be judged primarily by the permanent achievement of its economic aims.' The Christian, wrote Auden in 1933, in *Christianity and the Social Revolution,* must admit 'the necessity of violence, and judge the means by its end. He cannot deny, if he is honest, the reality of the class conflict'; and the social-democratic argument that the possessing classes 'will ever voluntarily abdicate' can no longer convince.

By the mid-Thirties this is the essence of the Popular Front case for accepting Stalin's leadership. And the omelette argument could be applied retrospectively to all history, not just to the present moment. 'When I read about Ivan the Terrible', said Dr Edith Summerskill in December 1935, addressing a Congress of Peace and Friendship with the U.S.S.R after a six-weeks' visit to the Soviet Union,

> I was not so much impressed by the fact that Ivan used to gouge out people's eyes but that he imported four German doctors into Russia. I also remember Peter the Great, and again the fact that he built Leningrad at the expense of millions of lives did not impress me so much as the fact that he introduced medicine into Russia.[35]

Millions of lives have ceased to matter much, by now. 'The world will likewise mark the admission by the Fabian Father', wrote Louis Fischer slyly in a *New Statesman* review of the Webbs' *Soviet Communism* (7 December 1935), 'that the end justifies the costs – and the means?' The Webbs, he had noticed with delight, had already accepted the Stalinist means.

5. *The individual no longer exists*; it is Party obedience that matters. More than one Communist, in the Thirties, echoes with a new enthusiasm Bertrand Russell's forebodings about blending Marxism

with the team spirit of the public school. Maurice Dobb, the Cambridge economist, after several visits to the Soviet Union, commended the 'tradition and discipline' of the Party as seen in government: 'a new race of men', he wrote warmly in his *Russia To-day and Tomorrow* (1930), 'disciplined by the machine and by labour, sometimes crude and always ruthless, but having vision and devotion...'.[36]

To achieve such power, total subservience is demanded of the faithful. A revolutionary, as Christopher Caudwell explained,

> must be a member of the revolutionary party. He must participate in its problems and help to form its tactics. He must execute the plans it has formed and which he had helped to form. He must co-operate in settling, and then accept and implement, the *party line.*[37]

This is no longer a matter for equivocation. The individual loses himself in obedience, he performs any act that is required of him. Marxism was held to have abolished the deepest foundations of individual morality. 'The entire structure of Communist ideology', wrote G. D. H. Cole in the *New Statesman* (20 April 1957), defending the Stalin years, rested on the just belief that 'there is in the real world no morality except class morality'. The duty of the individual, then, lies in total obedience in performing any act the Party requires: 'It was therefore justifiable and necessary for the proletariat to use any method and to take any action that would help it towards victory over its class-enemies'. The Marxist, with his faith in the inevitable laws of history, stands proudly outside morality altogether. No individual can matter; none can have rights.

6. *Violence is naïve, simple, authentic.* Often, as one reads the literature of the Thirties, one is reminded of Wordsworth and his leech-gatherer in 'Resolution and Independence', granting only that the Worker has by now imaginatively replaced the romantic wayfarer, peasant or child. Gide noted in his journal (March 1935) how, for many a bourgeois like himself who had never had to work for a living, it was impossible not to feel inferior in the presence of 'a simple workman'. The bourgeois feels small. Orwell, who was all the better at exposing these myths because he was himself, in some sense and in some moods, a victim of them, put it all unforgettably in the opening paragraphs of *Homage to Catalonia,* describing a young Italian volunteer to the Spanish Republic:

Something in his face deeply moved me. It was the face of a man who would commit murder and throw away his life for a friend. . . . There were both candour and ferocity in it; also the pathetic reverence that illiterate people have for their supposed superiors.

The romantic phenomenon the French call *ouvrièrisme* has no equivalent term in English, but it is among the deepest of emotions in the Thirties. Isherwood, a few years before, had seen the same vision in the Berlin of 1931, at a Communist meeting, and in *Mr Norris Changes Trains* (1935) he describes the excitement he took from the faces of a German audience of workers:

> They were listening to their own collective voice. At intervals they applauded it, with sudden, spontaneous violence. Their passion, their strength of purpose elated me. I stood outside it. One day, perhaps, I should be with it, but never of it.[38]

7. *Marxism means violence.* In the Thirties extermination seemed plainly required by Marxist doctrine. It was not just something you would do if it proved necessary. You knew it would prove necessary. The bourgeoisie, during and after the Revolution, would have to be eliminated. Some might be successfully re-educated; some might prove genuine revolutionaries themselves. But the fate of the millions who remained was not really in doubt. The literature of the Thirties can be outspoken about this, unlike most Marxist apologetics since the war. Bernard Shaw once prepared a speech called 'The Terrible Responsibility' soon after the October Revolution, and his notes run: '(1) Killing; (2) Inculcating the State morality in schools; signing death warrants; ordering troops to fire . . . a Socialist Government will have to do both.'[39] The orthodox Marxist position was that the ruling class would inevitably start violence, and Franco's invasion of Spain in 1936 seemed a classic exemplum of the principle; the workers would reply, answering violence with violence, and destroy their class enemies. John Strachey, in *The Theory and Practice of Socialism* (1936), accepts that the coming eradication of the middle class can only be bloody: 'We predict that, unfortunately, the process of that abolition will be accompanied by the same violence which today characterizes all the major activities of human life.' History demands it:

The historical record declares that no great change in the way of
life of human communities has hitherto been achieved without
the pains and travails of a birth process. Force, said Marx in a
famous phrase, has long been the midwife of every old society
pregnant with the new.[40]

The death warrant of a class has been made out, and it will be
executed: this is the warning openly made to the age. In Brecht's *Die
Massnahme* (1930), when the Communist agitators ask the Controller
whether they were right to murder an unreliable comrade, the
answer is to more questions than that:

> When they meet us, wherever it be,
> Let them know: the rulers
> Shall be exterminated.

The doctrine of extermination was simply held in that age, and
simply put.

★

The Stalinist intellectuals of the Thirties are nowadays something of
a joke. The Red Thirties, as somebody once remarked, gave place to
the red-faced Fifties; and the short-lived Marxist revival of the Sixties, deeply impressed as it was with its own myth of uniqueness, left
the whole question carefully unexplored. I reopen it here as a question of history, and of nothing else: whoever may have chanced to
survive, the age itself is forever dead and gone. My own judgement,
as a literary historian, is of documents rather than of men, of what
books and periodicals say.

But the literary evidence does not bear out the myths of innocence
and self-deception. It plainly suggests that poets and novelists in
that age were attracted to the most violent system on earth because
they knew it was that. Soviet dictatorship looked to them a highly
disciplined system that could and should conquer the world; the
God that Failed was a savage god. Between 1930 and 1939 many,
and perhaps most, British intellectuals under the age of fifty, and a
good many in other Western lands, knowingly supported what may
well have been the greatest act of mass murder in European history.

Even the accusing eye of the historian is bound to flicker in
the bright light of that assertion, and wish the evidence less good
than it is.

4 *The Literature of Fascism*

Was there ever a literature of fascism in Britain?

The question, once it is posed, needs to be made precise. I am not remotely concerned here with fascism as a term of abuse, but with an advocacy by men of letters of Mussolini after 1922, of Hitler after 1933, or of any similar dictator: the sole proviso being that advocacy should be of doctrines characteristic of those dictators. Anyone who praised Hitler in the Thirties, as Wyndham Lewis did, as 'essentially a man of peace', cannot reasonably be thought on that ground to qualify. The commitment in question is not only to a political leader but to a creed: one of central authority, a planned economy and a one-party state, often joined with a noisy contempt for Western democracy and Eastern communism; of racialism, more often than not; and of military virtue and the heroics of war.

I do not believe that any of the writers considered here can usefully be called fascist, at least during the period of their extended residence in Britain. But the answer cannot be an unequivocal No. This is a study in approximations: in how certain writers drew close to admiring a leader and his policies, or independently held views that resemble those policies. And these approximations belong to individuals, not to a group. The literary 'Right' between the wars was never a coterie or a single cause, not even briefly, as its opponents decidedly were. The British Union of Fascists, launched by Sir Oswald Mosley in October 1932, never occupied an intellectual role equivalent to that of the British Communist Party. The Right was wracked by ignorance of what was happening, as well as torturing uncertainties and sheer wilfulness. Every case is different: some are simply and forever unclassifiable. Wyndham Lewis, for example, defined his position in 1928 as 'partly communist and partly fascist, with a distinct streak of monarchism in my marxism, but at bottom anarchist with a healthy passion for order'.[1] Such men pose taxing problems for the political analyst, and with intent. They force each case to be considered separately.

★

In Britain, as in other Western democracies, an awareness of fascism hardly began until after Hitler's accession to power in January 1933. The March on Rome in October 1922 had not seemed to demand much analytical attention from intellectuals, and had only occasionally received it. Italy was not thought a vital force in European affairs, in any event, and there was no reason to see Mussolini for what, in the event, he proved to be – the first in a long line of new leaders who by 1940 would subjugate almost all of Continental Europe. He might as easily be the last of an old stock: one British historian, writing as a former Conservative Member of Parliament in about 1930, saw his doctrine as representing 'the idealism of Mazzini, combined with the practical statesmanship of Cavour and the heroic temper of Garibaldi'.[2] And Italy, in any case, was Italy: an everlasting charmer among nations, practised in manipulating and mitigating any political system that took possession of it by a humanising corruption and a beguilingly indolent life-style. It looked like no sort of power, whether industrial or military, and very far from a political inspiration. The most Mussolini could hope to stand for abroad in those early days was a joke in the best style; Cambridge undergraduates in the Twenties, so Isherwood reports, might call their terriers 'Musso' if they were rugger or rowing men.[3] But as a political phenomenon, fascism was simply not felt in the Twenties to be of European significance. And even if D. H. Lawrence, who died three years before the advent of Hitler, held views that could be seen to stand in a startling relationship to the new tide of thought on the Continent, nobody could seriously suppose him an admirer of any existing dictator. Before 1933 intellectual fascism is scarcely to be seen or heard in Britain.

What is more, the growth of National Socialism in German elections in the late Twenties and after, checked as it sometimes was, did not always appear to demand much attention either. Hitler might come to nothing: the British press more than once carried reports that he had shot his bolt. Or he might attain office only to be outwitted by cleverer and more experienced politicians than himself; or create a chaos from which others, probably the German Communist Party, could benefit. In 1933 G. D. H. and Margaret Cole, in their *Intelligent Man's Guide*, were still talking of Nazism as provisional. There was no reason that looked compelling to take fascism seriously before January 1933, or even for a year or two after that.

How did fascism look after Hitler's accession? One unexpected witness here is Richard Crossman, who in May 1933 published an anonymous article 'How Nazis Think' in his *New Oxford Outlook*. It was a report on a recent international student conference at Leyden attended by an official National Socialist delegation, 'at a time when all parties in England are united by the common bond of hatred for the new régime in Germany'. The author, who may have been Crossman himself, saw the young Nazis as morally earnest, 'like members of a Buchmanite group', and described how they 'consistently talked of the moral revolution' that had just happened in Germany, 'the destruction of materialism, the triumph of Idealism over Marxismus', condemning objectivity with one voice as 'a menace to political success'. Aryanism, as they preached it, meant the end of atomic individualism in favour of the state as an organism, as well as racial superiority, national unity and the recovery of lost lands. 'In fact, pure Spengler', the young Englishman comments knowingly; the Nazis have borrowed 'all the barbarism of Russian Communism' for 'precisely opposite ends'.

The new creed, however, did not clearly deserve the title of an intellectual system. Intelligent response was principally one of horror mingled with puzzlement; and only mystical explanations, like Jung's or D. H. Lawrence's, seemed to help towards understanding what had occurred. Fascism was a freak. No earlier system of political thought, whether conservative, liberal or Marxist, had predicted these bizarre events, and early interpretations have a hurried and anxious air. Hitler's final values, Crossman wrote a year later, in the *New Oxford Outlook* of November 1934, 'are not principles, are not indeed intellectual at all: they are emotional attitudes, metaphysical reactions', and the leader himself is 'an evangelist and a preacher' of organising genius, basing his doctrine on the paradox of 'conservative revolution'. At that early date, at least, Crossman did not consider fascism right-wing; he saw it rather as an ideal of economic planning akin to socialism: 'Hitler is conservatism incarnate. He is not a Fascist Dictator imposing a rational economic and social system upon a sullen majority. He is not a radical reformer.

... He is the expression of that deep-seated belief in authority, in paternalism, in the rule of the élite' – a belief that millions take for granted in France and Britain: more like Stanley Baldwin than Mussolini, in short.

This is not an isolated view. Julian Huxley, in a letter of 1933, at a time when he was moving rapidly towards his Communist commitment, fully accepted that fascism was a version of radical socialism, though an outrageously and dangerously crude one: '... a real menace to freedom of opinion and liberty of action ... a short cut towards the unified Socialized State which should be our goal. But its methods are so crude that it is likely to land us in war and social disaster while delaying real progress.' W. H. Auden, in *The Dance of Death* (1933), imagines an announcer broadcasting a call for a British Fascist revolution, at once anti-capitalist and anti-semitic: 'Down with the dictatorship of international capital', he shouts. 'The Anglo-Saxon race is in danger',[4] and they beat up a Jew. It was commonplace even among intellectual Marxists to acknowledge a connection, both logical and historical, between socialism and anti-semitism.

All this suggests that the international Communist 'explanation' of fascism as the last gasp of capitalism was not current in British socialist opinion as early as 1933–4, though it was to become almost universal soon after, in the age of the Popular Front. Crossman, Huxley and Auden see fascism at first glance as an outrageously brutal version of socialism, risking a sacred cause by enforcing state planning before the masses are ready to accept it. More detached observers echo this interpretation. As early as 1916 the young T. S. Eliot, already an exponent of the French royalist Charles Maurras and his Action Française, had remarked how much socialism had in common with royalism and other doctrines of conservative leadership.[5] They arose out of a desire for order and for planning, and the socialist origins of Mussolini and Hitler were soon to make that parallel inescapable. Harold Nicolson, on a visit to Rome with Mosley in January 1932, tells in his diary how he spent the day there reading Fascist pamphlets, and concluded that Mussolini and his followers had 'turned the whole country into an army', though he was puzzled to know how far, if at all, it had affected the lives of ordinary Italians. 'It is certainly a socialist experiment in that it destroys individuality. It also destroys liberty.'[6]

Expositions of the Corporate State, or of Mosley's 'Organic State', abound in the Britain of the Thirties, but they grope in undisguised bafflement among doctrines still felt to be too new to be easily assimilated. The few certainties they can offer were these: that fascism is a new and violent version of socialism; that it hates individual liberty and all assumptions concerning the Rights of Man; that it is opposed to materialism and international finance; and that, in contrast with the middle-aged Bolsheviks governing Russia and the elderly statesmen who headed the Western democracies, it is a dogma about the young, by the young and for the young. The Fascist hymn of Italy was aptly felt to be entitled 'Giovinezza'. 'The sands are running out', one British observer wrote in 1932: 'The old order may yet find itself replaced by some sort of Fascism. For the history of our times will be woven on the loom of Youth.'[7] An odder view is offered by Isherwood, who saw fascism in the late Thirties as an outcome of an intensely seductive 'homosexual romanticism' – an aspect of youthful idealism neglected in the West, he believed, though Fascist rulers 'profoundly understand and make use of just these phantasies and longings'.[8]

But it cannot be said that the British intellectual reaction to fascism by the mid-Thirties was notably perceptive – still less that it touched many chords among the persecuted in central Europe itself, or showed much intimate awareness of the dangers to be faced there.

An almost forgotten exception deserves to be recorded. Ernest Barker, a Cambridge professor, attacked National Socialism in a Hamburg lecture in December 1936 in a manner at once delicate, eloquent and bold. In an epilogue to his *Oliver Cromwell and the English People* (1937) entitled 'The English Puritan Revolution and the German National Socialist Revolution', Barker plainly hints at an analogy between Cromwell and Hitler (whom he skilfully does not name), but only for their common faculty of drawing divided nations together by 'a unity of fundamentals'. The contrasts between them seemed to him more striking: Cromwell 'never thought of himself as a leader or hero',[9] and his impulse was religious, not racial. What is more, 'the Puritans generally were good internationalists', at least so far as Protestant Europe was concerned: 'There is nothing physical in this conception. There is no belief in blood or race.'[10] Precisely because they used force, and to excess, the Puritans left England with 'the legacy of hatred of a standing army; the legacy of a rooted dislike of compulsory godliness; the legacy of contempt for . . . cant and hypocrisy'. And in the end, they gave England liberty.[11] This must have been the most subtle critique of National Socialism addressed to the Germany of 1936; and it was an Englishman who had the wit and courage to write it.

★

An Edwardian generation of writers, meanwhile, was still to be heard in Britain: Russell, Wells, Shaw, Chesterton and Belloc; all born in another century, and all well past their youth before the advent of Hitler and the outbreak of Civil War in Spain three years later. Bertrand Russell, though impressed by Marxism, remained staunchly unimpressed by Lenin and Stalin after a visit to Russia, and was contemptuous of the new Fascist leaders; H. G. Wells, without being a Marxist, admired Lenin as a man of power; and Bernard Shaw, a classic instance of the power-worshipping literary intellectual, was an eager disciple both of Marxism and of Stalin's regime, at times of Mussolini and even, in an occasional aside, of Hitler.

Meanwhile their Catholic opponents were proposing a rival faith. Chesterton's editorials in *GK's Weekly*, which he edited down to his death in 1936, are sceptical of National Socialism but less than hostile: anti-Prussian rather than anti-German, and contemptuous of racial ideas largely as instances of the sin of pride. Belloc's articles, written for his friend's journal, strike a more acrid note than Chesterton's. Moscow engineers every revolution on earth, he argues in August 1936; and Moscow is

> only a symbolic word for a group of men which is cosmopolitan and largely Jewish, with the Jewish intensity of purpose – whether humanistic and Messianic, or devoted to power or vengeance – the Jewish ability to act in secret, the Jewish indifference to property and national ideals, the fierce Jewish sense of justice, and above all the Jewish tenacity.

It 'colours the whole affair' of Bolshevism. All this comes pretty close to the Berlin line; and later editorials express concern over a lasting victory for Moscow in Spain, and see nationalism – whether Spanish or German – as merely a passing phenomenon. In a new introduction of 1937 to *The Jews,* which had been first published in 1922,

Belloc reiterated his claim that communism was essentially Jewish: 'Jews as such are not Communists, but the modern Communist movement was inspired and is directed by Jews.'[12] Belloc saw strife in Spain as a religious war, while 'the Government at Berlin is seriously occupied with fighting a European revolution'.[13] But he was still unready to support the letter of anti-semitism as practised in the new Germany, only its spirit; and he remained temperamentally opposed as a Catholic to the northern and Protestant peoples. The whole affair was all 'racial vanity gone mad',[14] he concluded, since the Aryanism of the Germans was anyhow unprovable; and in any case Berlin had failed to make itself the rallying-point the world needs against Jewish communism. Though closer to National Socialism than Chesterton ever was, and highly tolerant of its foreign adventures, he stops short of endorsing its policies at home.

★

The new men, meanwhile – Pound, Eliot, Wyndham Lewis – had by the mid-Thirties adopted a series of political positions that look bafflingly diverse. Some elements of a new intellectual conservatism or nostalgic radicalism were already visible before 1914. Pound had already praised Provençal poetry in *The Spirit of Romance* (1910) in glowing terms as the creation of 'a democratic aristocracy',[15] an élite of new talents and a patrician order boldly revivified from the ranks. But in some ways the dictators of the Thirties, when they emerged, embarrassed more literary minds than they excited, even when a doctrinal kinship might have attracted intellectuals into their ranks. Wyndham Lewis had supported Italian fascism in *The Art of Being Ruled* (1926), it is true, and wrote two books in modified and facetious praise of Hitler; one of them – *Hitler* (1931) – before the seizure of power; and he condoned the Italian invasion of Abyssinia in 1935 and sided with Franco in 1936. But the chief thrust of his argument was anti-French: an hostility to the Versailles treaty rather than a positive sympathy with National Socialism. In the mid-Twenties, like others, he had seen fascism as a modern variant of socialism, and one probably better suited to nations like Britain than Bolshevism. 'For anglo-saxon countries as they are constituted today', he wrote, 'some modified form of fascism would probably be the best'.[16]

'The Men of 1914' (in Wyndham Lewis's phrase) were to pass

through a succession of moods that Pound, their chief inspirer, was later to summarise: first, the *Blast* group of the 1910s, youthful and iconoclastic; second, and in the Twenties, a new conservatism, 'the sorting out, the *rappel à l'ordre*'; and third, 'the new synthesis, the totalitarian'.[17] In Pound's case, the third stage was to involve him in 125 broadcasts from Rome between December 1941 and July 1943, for which he was later detained and tried for treason as an American citizen. A fourth stage can now be added, one of remorse. 'The worst mistake I made', he told Allen Ginsberg in 1967, in abject old age, 'was that stupid, suburban prejudice of anti-semitism.'[18]

W. B. Yeats, meanwhile, had independently anticipated much of Pound's call to order. Long before Pound settled in England in 1908, Yeats had adopted a romantic version of Irish nationalism as his own, in old Fenian style; he had believed in revolution long before Pound or Lewis, and in authoritarian government long before the March on Rome. In Mussolini he was to see congenial resemblances, but never a simple focus for his own loyalties. By aspiration and conviction he was an aristocrat, if hardly one in fact, and fascism was too vulgar a phenomenon to attract him consistently and for long. Snobbery, that supreme discriminator, always held him back where the fervour of political conviction might have pressed him onwards into a final commitment. His distrust of De Valera made him long for a political Messiah for Ireland: and by July 1933, months after Hitler had followed De Valera into office, he joyfully saw politics as suddenly 'heroic', with the exciting prospect of an aristocratic putsch:

> A Fascist opposition is forming behind the scenes to be ready should some tragic situation develop. I find myself constantly urging the despotic rule of the educated classes as the only end of our troubles. (Let all this sleep in your ear.) I know half a dozen men any one of whom may be Caesar – or Catiline,

adding that Ireland has the great strength of preferring action to thought: 'There is so little in our stocking that we are ready at any moment to turn it inside out; and how can we not feel emulous when we see Hitler juggling with his sausage of stocking?' Emulous on his own account, he eagerly devised a flag for the Irish Blueshirts, and excitedly waited for an Irish revolution that would answer the laws of history: 'History is very simple – the rule of the many; then the rule of the few, day and night, night and day forever, while in small disturbed nations day and night race.'[19]

Ten days later, in another letter, he was to hail as leader General O'Duffy, a former police chief who had just been greeted by his Blueshirts with Fascist salutes and who had listened patiently and at length to Yeats's 'anti-democratic philosophy'. But Yeats's hesitations at the prospect of an Irish dictatorship are as characteristic as his hopes for a political Messiah: 'Italy, Poland, Germany, then perhaps Ireland. Doubtless I shall hate it (though not so much as I hate Irish democracy).'[20] Soon he was to long for Franco's victory in Spain, if only to embarrass a British empire he had grown in his last years to detest with a mounting obsession.

T. S. Eliot, years earlier, had pre-empted the title of this essay with an article on 'The Literature of Fascism' in the *Criterion* of December 1928. It was a review of five books from various hands by a forty-year-old poet who called himself 'interested in political ideas, but not in politics'. By the late Twenties, Eliot was an Anglican, a royalist and a British patriot, and he openly regarded both bolshevism and fascism, except as ways of running such remote territories as Russia and Italy, as mere 'humbug'. His deepest political allegiances were still with Charles Maurras's Action Française, which he had come to admire during his student year in the Paris of 1910–11, and its doctrine of an executive monarchy.

By the age of forty, Eliot's political views form one of the most amazing intellectual hybrids known to any age. Always a conservative, he was by 1928 a highly individual version of a French monarchist turned Englishman, with mental vestiges of a native America. He always forswore panaceas: 'Order and authority are good: I believe in them as wholeheartedly as I think one should believe in any single idea', and the reality of fascism could not attract him much, since to an idealist philosopher grounded in Bergson and F. H. Bradley all reality in its nature was suspect: 'Both Russian communism and Italian fascism seem to me to have died as political ideas in becoming political facts.'[21] Months later, in reply to critics, he restated his position more clearly. Fascism and communism are broadly similar systems: at least they reveal a 'family likeness'.[22] But they are also inadequate in similar ways; both are 'well-meaning revolts against "capitalism", but revolts which do not appear to me to get to the bottom of the matter'.[23] He is still prepared, with manifold qualifications, to take sides: 'I confess a preference for fascism in practice. . . . The fascist form of unreason is less remote from my own than that of the communists.' But his real allegiances were French. 'England is a Latin country', he had announced early in his editorship of the *Criterion*,[24] and the real task was to promote Maurras as an influence upon the British political mind, an influence he believed not yet begun.

That moulding force upon Eliot's own mind, like so much about him, is hard to summarise: a sense of thought as bodily, even visceral, as well as cerebral; a longing for what Maurras had called a *pays réel* in place of the *pays légal* of industrial democracy, or a love of roots and a horror of cosmopolitanism; a fear and a contempt, directly consequent upon that, of atomised industrial life and of the head-counting rituals of democracy; and a deep and fearful awareness of the relations between belief and action. But it was Paris, not Berlin, that preserved his deepest allegiances, and the cultivated life of a political group there that demonstrated in the streets but never saw office or shook off its profound pessimism over the state of modern life.

A British patriot in the Second World War, he had by his last years embraced a scepticism of a kind that made the British Conservative Party his natural, though never quite his ideal, home. 'We move always', he once told them, 'if not in the dark, in a twilight, with imperfect vision, constantly mistaking one object for another, imagining distant obstacles where none exists, and unaware of some fatal menace close at hand.'[25] That is perhaps a better description of his audience than he meant it to be. But no government, and no ruling party, ever commanded the loyalty of his mind. He was too fastidious to salute success.

★

Many of the intellectuals considered here were receptive, or potentially receptive, to fascism well before 1933. What did that receptivity mean? I propose here to study that vague and untidy thing, an intellectual predisposition: a state of mind that held the loyalties of intelligent men before the advent of Hitler, and influenced their attitudes to the dictators when they came.

In an extended passage in *Blasting and Bombardiering* (1937),

Wyndham Lewis set out to explain at length how it was that the doctrine of Original Sin had come to look important to T. E. Hulme and his friends before the First World War. Familiar as it must be accounted, the doctrine suddenly seemed a telling answer to H. G. Wells's facile optimism; it was a way of putting man at last in his proper place. Lewis, who quotes Mussolini approvingly as an exponent of the principles of authority, praises communism and fascism equally as 'purgatives': 'Both are good as such. Both give the Poor a run for their money or for their lack of it, both clear the way for personal ambition or against impersonal birth. Both shake out or shake off a lot of dead matter.' To that extent, he argues gaily, Karl Marx had had much the same salutary function as the Marx brothers. 'The world needed badly a bit of fresh air and it's got it. And the windows have been blown out. We're nearer to nature than we've been for a long time.'[26]

The influence of Hulme, who died in battle in 1917, has always been difficult to define. He was perhaps the first Englishman to follow the French lead of associating classicism in literature with conservatism in politics and a respect for ecclesiastical restraint.[27] Unoriginal as the components of his system are, the totality was felt to be potent, though Hulme's own conservatism was never more than tentative. His was a doctrine of human limitation, hostile to all doctrines of the perfection or perfectibility of man, and deeply convinced that such doctrines were the vulgar essence of romanticism. Man, as he put it in his posthumously published *Speculations* (1924), is 'essentially limited and imperfect' and Original Sin is the supreme symbol of his limitation.[28] All this is very unlike the boundless futuristic optimism of Mussolini, Hitler and Mosley. But it is less unlike the second-order and conservative fascism of Franco, pre-war Poland and some Balkan rulers in the Thirties, or of the Action Française in Paris. Conservative fascism, paradoxical as it is, existed in literature before it existed territorially. Hulme had attacked the tradition of Rousseau and demanded 'the subordination of men to certain absolute values'[29] to compensate for what he conceived of as the imminent breakdown of humanism, and in his *Speculations* he praised Maurras and the Action Française as well as Bergson; in fact he uncritically accepts Maurras's glib identification of romanticism with the French Revolution and political liberalism, picturing it as slush and 'spilt religion'.[30]

But like Pound, Hulme is also a relentless *avant-gardiste*, so that the literary Right he inspired was from the start artistically radical as well as politically nostalgic; and by a supreme paradox, of which Eliot's *The Waste Land* is the supreme monument, its nostalgia and its radicalism were one. Hulme's own dedication to the strenuous task of being fashionable was public and outspoken. Intellectual fashions grow old and decay, he held, like other organisms; and an intelligent man has a duty to look modern, if only because the *élan vital* is the motive force of the evolutionary process. Hulme was by temperament a passionate radical, and worshipped action, not only from afar: '*Passion is action*, and without action but a child's anger'.[31] He approvingly quotes revolutionary socialists like Proudhon and Sorel, the last of whom he translated; and *Speculations* ends with a personal declaration in favour of egalitarian socialism. His memory survived through the Twenties and Thirties as the dead Messiah of the New Right, but only by dint of selective interpretation and a convenient amnesia. His name, in any case, was not famed enough after his early death to give intellectual conservatism much sense of coherence.

As a movement, intellectual conservatism in modern Britain has lacked everything that a movement needs: a meeting-place, a manifesto, a promised land. As often as not, it could not even see fascism as an international force. Pound, when he lauded Mussolini in the early Thirties as the new Marx, insulted Hitler in the same treatise for his hysterical yawping.[32] Evelyn Waugh praised Mussolini's conquest of Ethiopia in 1935–6 for bringing civilisation to a dark continent, and mocked cheerfully at the spectacle of Western socialists supporting the Emperor Haile Selassie;[33] but he never supported Hitler. Roy Campbell, a Catholic convert and noisy anti-semite who (if his own wild claims can be believed) fought for Franco after 1936 on escaping from prison in Toledo, saw little in Mussolini to interest him and nothing in Hitler. The Spanish War, in his eyes, was a crusade against atheistical bolshevism, not to mention the 'protestantism gone bad' of Left intellectuals who indulge themselves sentimentally in 'the filth or famine of others'.[34] Waugh and Campbell were avowed eccentrics, and eager to be seen as such. But much the same could be said of Chesterton, Belloc, Pound, Eliot and Wyndham Lewis. They were all men with an intense awareness of their own singularity in the world, and all contemptuous of the well-drilled uniformity of the intellectual Left – of what Eliot derisively called a tendency to 'scramble for salvation' by 'taking a ticket'.[35] Communism looked too easy an option to them: the Thirties way of marching in step.

And yet, as much as any Communist, the conservatives longed for order; and if any common and consistent factor is to be sought, then it can only be the doctrine that the individual should acknowledge his limits and humble himself to a master. Though there could be no agreement about which master, the principle itself was not in dispute. Pound was to summarise that mood unforgettably after the war, as a prisoner awaiting trial for treason, in his eighty-first canto; and the lines resound heroically from such a man in so extreme a misfortune:

> . . . Pull down thy vanity: it is not man
> Made courage, or made order, or made grace,
> Pull down thy vanity, I say pull down.

It was not the Left alone, he must have hauntingly felt at that moment, that had dared too far and trusted its judgement too confidently. Evelyn Waugh, just before the war, had put the same matter less succinctly in prose, strengthened in its conservatism at that moment by a visit to a turbulent and violent Mexico. He wrote boldly in *Robbery under Law* (1939):

> I believe that man is by nature an exile and will never be self-sufficient or complete on this earth; that his chances of happiness and virtue, here, remain more or less constant through the centuries, . . . not much affected by the political and economic conditions in which he lives; that the balance of good and ill tends to revert to a norm. . . . I believe in government. . . . I believe that inequalities of wealth and position are inevitable. . . . I believe in nationality. . . .[36]

Mexico strengthened his stand as a conservative, as the chaos of the Spanish Republic had just done; and he entered the war against Hitler in 1939 with a good heart, to lose it only when the German invasion of Russia in June 1941 made Stalin a British ally and the struggle against atheism an enterprise forever compromised.

★

And yet, one may guess, there was an almost necessary reason why Pound's view and Waugh's could find no leader to be shared with others of like mind. The conservative mind feeds on nostalgia: its myth is always of a better time long past that can never be lived again. Any choice the conservative makes, for this reason, can only be in a mood of avoidance and out of fear of something worse. He thinks, speaks and votes against dangers, real or imagined; he changes his leaders lightly, having given full allegiance to none. No present age can hope to mean more to him than the shadow of dead and departed times. History itself has betrayed modern man simply by making him modern; as Dryden once remarked, 'all comes wasted to us'; the best of life and thought has already been lived and conceived. Expatriates like Pound and Eliot were in a double quandary: they had crossed the Atlantic as to a promised land, and then found to their grief that they had to construct for themselves a world of mind out of the detritus of a European civilisation already in collapse.

'These fragments I have shored against my ruins' Eliot concluded sadly in *The Waste Land*. No actuality, after that disappointment, could satisfy minds so ideally constituted. Their love was ultimately for a remote idea of order: the China of Confucius, the artistic comradeship of the Provençal troubadour, Elizabeth and Leicester – any idea that could defy and 'pull down' a tumultuously competitive and strident Now. The living, thriving and all-conquering dictators of the Thirties, for just that reason, could not satisfy them for long, if at all. They had not yet won for themselves the unimpeachable dignity that only time and history can confer.

5 | *Left and Right*

In October 1931 Lloyd George advised Herbert Samuel, the Liberal leader, not to ally himself with the Conservatives. 'If I am to die', he said, 'I would rather die fighting on the Left.' On the way home Samuel noticed a road sign: 'Keep Left – One Way Only', and quoted it approvingly to Lloyd George as an omen. And the next day he was to resist the call for a joint National Government manifesto at the coming general election.[1]

The story illustrates how political language and slogans can affect the decision of statesmen, even events themselves: none more than a system of language like Left, Right and Centre, which claims to offer a descriptive model for every shade of opinion. In any competition for moderation, men will hurry to what is called the Centre; for purity, to what they suppose to be one end or another of the spectrum; hence the progressive asseveration of *pas d'ennemis à la gauche*. In the shortlived Portuguese Constituent Assembly of 1975, in a revolutionary atmosphere, no party wished to be found sitting on the right of the Chamber. But handedness or laterality is recent as a metaphor in British politics. How and why did Westminster, and journalistic and literary London, come to accept the terminology of Left and Right?

The Victorians rarely used Left, Right and Centre of themselves. In the nineteenth century such terms were seen as Continental in origin and application, and above all as French. It is exceptional to find them in British political debate before the present century. An historical dictionary, in a volume published in 1908, gives only one political sense to Left: 'In continental legislatures, the section of members who occupy seats on the left side of the chamber', meaning those who hold 'relatively liberal or democratic opinions'.[2] Derivative terms are even later, and probably belong to the years between the wars. 'Leftism' is recorded no earlier than 1930, 'left-wing' only in 1922, and 'leftist' in 1924.[3] For the British before 1914 all this was essentially a matter for foreigners. W. S. Gilbert's sentry in *Iolanthe* (1882), who believed that a man from birth is 'either a little Liberal, or else a little Conservative', is offering a crude version of what most people believed, and there were plenty of qualifying terms like 'advanced' or 'moderate' to refine these appellations. Since those two parties dominated parliamentary politics till 1918, there was no clear reason to adopt a Continental terminology until that year – just as there is none to this day that would require it in the United States or Canada.

But long before the outbreak of the Second World War the new terminology had plainly come to dominate the intelligent analysis of British politics; and by 1939 it had entered the bloodstream of ordinary electoral debate. The probable period for the assimilation of these terms, then, is the 1920s.

Why did it happen? The simplest answer, and in many ways a sufficient one, is that the advent of Labour in 1918 as a principal party of state made a Continental terminology look natural and even imperative. Though older than socialism, it had as a terminology already absorbed something of that European doctrine into its system. But a new terminology cannot be adopted without dislocation, and that dislocation is not to language alone. Ideas, as Leopardi once remarked, are 'enclosed and almost bound in words, like jewels in a ring'; and they cannot be separated from a familiar setting and remain the same. If socialism is to be judged to stand to the left of liberalism, for example, then the Liberal can no longer plausibly claim to represent radical opinion, and he must grow accustomed to hearing himself called a moderate. And these considerations of context and setting apply equally to any future abandonment of Left and Right as terms of political description. Most people would have to start thinking all over again. And thinking is hard. That is why abandonment is in practice so difficult. Merely to question the spectrum theory of politics is by now to mark oneself out as an eccentric; to deny it is to convict oneself in most quarters of a fondness for paradox, at the best, and at the worst an inclination to verbal double-dealing. But it may help at the outset to weaken the

Superstition of the Spectrum by recalling how recent a concept in British politics it is. Most people in modern British parliamentary history since the Reform Act of 1832 have done without it entirely.

A polarity is always attractive. For one thing, it is simple. The Ancients, for instance, believed in the moral superiority of Right over Left, and often associated them with the sacred and the profane.[4] Anybody can understand this sort of thing in a moment, and anybody can learn to use it. But it is beginning to grow increasingly clear, even to the incurious, that such terms as Left and Right now offer a highly inaccurate reflection of political realities, and in many ways a gravely misleading one. Some of the strains of spectrum analysis are becoming acute. A referendum on Europe in 1975 that put Mr Enoch Powell and Mr Michael Foot in one camp, and Mr Wilson, Mr Heath and Mr Thorpe in another, raised questions about the use of language even as it settled the issue of Community membership. On many urgent choices, by the Seventies, the spectrum had ceased to work. It does not assist analysis: it does not even describe. A terminology that has functioned in Britain for half a century has now largely ceased to perform its task, or at least to perform it accurately.

★

How, at its best, did it once work? The high point of its acceptance was the 1930s, and it would be instructive to present the literary world of those years as two rival teams in an imaginary game, with the year 1936–7 as the chief point of division. Each list here is chronological by date of birth; and since Right and Left in politics have nothing by now to do with laterality or handedness, they may stand reversed on the page as shown overleaf.

Hulme is admitted to the Right list here because, though killed in action in 1917, his influential *Speculations* did not appear as a posthumous manifesto until 1924. Hilaire Belloc (1870–1953) and G. K. Chesterton (1874–1936) might be added to the Catholic Right between the wars as survivors from another literary epoch; and Pound is included because of the decisive years of 1908–20, which he largely spent in London before migrating to Paris and Italy.

On the Left, a host of names could be added with a variety of qualifications: Sean O'Casey (1884–1964), who mixed Marxism with Irish nationalism; Hugh MacDiarmid (b. 1892), who mixed it with Scottish; Cyril Connolly (1903–74), a largely unpolitical writer whose allegiances were on that side, at least in the Thirties; his friend George Orwell (1903–50), who attacked the literary Left from within it; Graham Greene (b. 1904), who turned Catholic in the late 1920s to become, as Orwell perceptively predicted, 'our first Catholic fellow traveller';[5] Aldous Huxley (1894–1963), a pacifist of late Bloomsbury affiliations; and novelists such as Rex Warner and Edward Upward.

RIGHT	LEFT
W. B. Yeats, 1865–1939	Bloomsbury, etc.: Leonard
P. Wyndham Lewis,	and Virginia Woolf,
1882–1957	Maynard Keynes, Lytton
T. E. Hulme, 1883–1917	Strachey, E. M. Forster,
D. H. Lawrence, 1885–1930	Bertrand Russell . . .
Ezra Pound, 1885–1972	Cecil Day Lewis, 1904–72
T. S. Eliot, 1888–1965	Christopher Isherwood, b.
T. E. Lawrence, 1888–1935	1904
Roy Campbell, 1901–57	William Empson, b. 1906
Evelyn Waugh, 1903–66	W. H. Auden, 1907–73
	Louis MacNeice, 1907–63
	Stephen Spender, b. 1909

These opposing teams prompt some wider reflections about the literary world of the Thirties.

1. The Right was not, in the literary sense, less distinguished than the Left: rather the contrary. This remains arguable even if one deletes Hulme and both of the Lawrences, who were all dead by the mid-Thirties. This conclusion would have surprised the age itself. The dominance of the Left in universities and literary London was powerfully sensed and widely accepted at the time; and by the end of the decade the Left was often felt to be in total possession. 'There is now no intelligentsia that is not in some sense "left" ', wrote Orwell in 1940, adding that the last right-wing intellectual had perhaps been T. E. Lawrence, who had been killed in a road accident in 1935.[6] But Orwell had to change his mind a few years later, and warned in 1943 against the dangerous mistake socialists had made in 'ignoring what one might call the neo-reactionary school of writers'.[7] It was a mistake he had until recently made himself. And yet the available facts had not changed: Orwell had always known about Yeats and Eliot and Waugh. Though the literary strength of the Right in the Thirties now looks massive – it included after all the

two greatest poets in English of the first half of the century – it could escape an attentive observer at the time altogether. It is interesting to ask why.

2. Orwell's mistake can be better understood if it is realised how enormously the literary Left outnumbered the Right in a strictly quantitative sense. More extensive lists on both sides would make this clearer. The best documented confrontation of opinion of the time is provided by the *Left Review,* which in December 1937 published replies to its questionnaire on the Civil War in Spain as *Authors Take Sides on the Spanish War.* Out of 148 contributors, 100 declared for the Spanish Republic; only 5, including Evelyn Waugh and Edmund Blunden, were for Franco; 16, including Eliot, Pound, Charles Morgan and H. G. Wells, were either neutral or disinclined to commit themselves in an alien context. If 1936–7 is accepted as the Great Divide in the Right–Left struggle, then the numerical superiority of the literary Left in that year was massive, and it would have been easy to exaggerate it into a unanimity. Orwell was not alone in being over-impressed by the spectacle. The enormous success of Victor Gollancz's Left Book Club, founded in 1936,[8] and the more modest performance of the Right Book Club, founded soon after in rivalry by Ernest Benn (Mr Tony Benn's uncle), confirms that preponderance.

3. The literary Marxist is usually younger than most members of the Right by a whole generation: he was commonly born in the first decade of the century, his opponents in the 1880s. The contest of the Thirties smacks strongly of a generation struggle.

4. Throughout the inter-war years, and especially after 1936, there was a marked absence of literary enthusiasm for parliamentary ideas. The exceptions chiefly include survivors of the Bloomsbury Group, which was politically Liberal–Labour. The Woolfs belonged to the Labour Party, Keynes to the Liberal – and so probably did Forster, who once ruefully remarked near the end of a long life that he had never once voted for a successful parliamentary candidate. But Forster abandoned fiction in the Twenties, and there is strikingly little literary new blood in the three political parties in the Thirties. Under the patronage of A. G. Macdonell the Liberal Book Club published Osbert Sitwell, Augustus John, Maynard Keynes, Gilbert Murray and A. A. Milne, among others, and its list included Joyce Cary's *Power in Men* (1939); but it was quickly overtaken by the outbreak of war. Galsworthy, whose views had been reformist

without party allegiance, died on 31 January 1933, a few hours after Hitler took power in Germany. That event meant something like the end of non-commitment for a number of years, and it made moderation difficult. In 1940, in 'Inside the Whale', Orwell was to raise the possibility again. But the intervening years had left few writers unattached. Intellectuals tended to extremes; the mass parties were moderate, almost of necessity: that familiar contrast could hardly have been clearer than in that age. It was intellectuals, by and large, who were attracted by foreign dictatorships, not ordinary men.

The uncommitted – in the sense of those not publicly committed to a political stance – make a heterogeneous list. There is James Joyce (1882–1941), who lived abroad from 1904; Ivy Compton-Burnett (1892–1969), whose novels are conservative by implication, but only in that sense; Robert Graves (b. 1895), a social democrat of the Twenties who spent most of his life after 1929 in Spain; and Dylan Thomas (1913–52), strenuously unpolitical as a poet. By the mid-Thirties the Centre was weak; the uncommitted, doubtless by choice, scattered.

5. The Left are more upper-class in origin than the Right. 'MacSpaunday', as Roy Campbell derisively called them – MacNeice, Spender, Auden, Day Lewis and the rest – might almost be said, in all essentials, to have led the same early life, and it was a life strikingly superior in its social advantages. One could draw an identikit portrait of it: upper-professional-class parentage, with a bishop for father, or professor, or editor; preparatory school and a well-known public school; Oxford or Cambridge, usually the former; a period of schoolmastering and travelling; a first slim volume of verse, or a novel, and entry into London literary life, with a little reviewing; and disillusion, even emigration, by 1939.

The Right, by contrast, were not of dazzling social origin, though Waugh's upbringing exceptionally resembles that of a young Marxist in many respects. They were of barely middle-class parentage, or not even British; their education was outside the privileged confines of southern English life; and they often developed later, or endured a longer and less conventional route to fame. But there could be no clear and contrasting identikit portrait of the Right. It is not a set or a coterie between the wars, and it lacks a characteristic life-style based on a community of friendship or even acquaintance. Hulme and Eliot, for example, probably never met,[9] and 'the Men of 1914' did not survive the war as a group and were always disparate as personalities. Pound and Eliot ceased to be intimates in the Twenties, and neither of the Lawrences was a part of the circle. This, too, helps to explain Orwell's mistake: the Right may have existed powerfully in the literary world of the Thirties, but it did not exist as an entity. The Left, by contrast, was uniformed in its opinions and even its habits – a uniformity Orwell never tired of deriding: 'they take their cookery from Paris and their opinions from Moscow'. He might have added that some took their sexual habits from pre-Hitler Berlin, and their gestures, conversational style and high-pitched laughter from a cocktail-party tradition of the jazz age. They were a set and a world. But there is no life-style characteristic of the Right.

6. The Marxists are more native than the Right: all were born and educated in the British Isles. By contrast, the Right after 1918 looks cosmopolitan. Yeats returned to Ireland and served as a senator in the Irish Free State – unlike the Irish Marxist O'Casey, who chose Devon. Pound and Eliot were born and largely educated in the United States. Wyndham Lewis was born off the coast of Nova Scotia in a yacht, of American father and English mother, and though brought up in London suburbs and educated at Rugby and the Slade School of Art, he spent most of the first decade of the century as an artist in Paris. D. H. Lawrence married a German and chose to live abroad after the war. Roy Campbell was a South African; and T. E. Lawrence, though brought up in Oxford, was to create for himself an exotic immortality as Lawrence of Arabia.

The Left, then, was not only socially superior to the Right, and younger, and more of a kind; it was also more British. If you were fairly well-bred and expensively educated, born in the first decade of the twentieth century and of a literary bent, then your chances of not being a Marxist by the mid-Thirties were low.

7. The Left had a party, the Communist; and a promised land, the Soviet Union: at least all that was true by 1936. Trotskyism did not flourish in literary London as it did in New York. But the Right had neither a single party nor a promised land. Pound admired Mussolini's Italy, and chose to live there throughout his middle years; and Campbell admired Franco's Spain. But Eliot, a Francophile and still more an Anglophile, could see no dictator worth much of his loyalty; and Wyndham Lewis, though he wrote two books in modified praise of Hitler as a man of peace, praised him for virtues no one would now think of as Nazi, and sought no haven in Germany. The Left marched in step, intellectually speaking – at

least for a time. The Right between the wars never did that.

★

Neither side had any doubt what the issue between them was about. The Left, both would have agreed, loved the future, the Right the past; and the difference was seen by both sides as one between moving forward and moving back.

The Communist measures the future, the Elect fear the past,

as a minor poet of the Left put it succinctly.[10] The Right would not have disagreed. 'Dreariest of prospects', Evelyn Waugh once remarked of the future, imagining himself in the saddle of Wells's Time Machine: 'I should set the engine slow astern. To hover gently back through centuries . . . would be the most exquisite pleasure of which I can conceive.'[11]

That hovering back is the hallmark of the literary Right between the wars. Eliot's *The Waste Land* (1922) contrasts a vulgar or trivial present with one heroic past after another; Yeats in *The Tower* (1928) and *Words for Music* (1932) called the modern world to account through bright images of a vanished Byzantium; and Pound in his critical essays and in the *Cantos* invoked the troubadours of the Middle Ages among a host of critical witnesses. Explaining what he saw as the 'real issues' of the war in Spain in 1936, Roy Campbell put the matter in the bluntest terms:

> There could be no compromise in this war between the East and the West, between Credulity and Faith, between irresponsible innovation (which catches all 'intellectuals' once they have been hereditarily derailed) and tradition, between the emotions (disguised as reason) and the intelligence.[12]

Past versus present, tradition versus innovation: these were the stark alternatives supposed to underlie the inescapable choice between Right and Left.

★

Neither side, among men of letters, seems to have seen fascism as a modern radical force, and that is odd. An international theory that dubbed fascism the last phase of capitalism was hastily concocted in Communist circles in the Twenties to explain its sudden emergence. It was an ideologically embarrassing phenomenon, since Marx had failed to predict it; and though the explanation lacked credibility and even consistency, it took universal possession of the Left, and was not much questioned by the Right. Lenin had 'explained' imperialism as the last phase of capitalism; but it is doubtful if, in an overheated atmosphere, any comrade noticed that the orthodox explanation of fascism implied that Lenin had been mistaken. Imperialism or fascism: they cannot both have been last. But all theories about the end of the world need to justify that world's stubborn capacity to survive, and Marxists have always been fertile with reasons why the advent of the millennium must be briefly delayed. The German Communist Party tried to explain its defeat in the general election of September 1930 by telling its followers that, while the National Socialists were in fact the agents of finance-capital, many workers had been misled into voting for them as a protest against the system: 'Fascism is the last card of the German bourgeoisie, which it is now playing against the threat of worker-revolution.'[13] The English literary Left echoed this style of explanation for years with exemplary obedience. Fascism, wrote Harold Laski a few years later, is 'simply the expedient adopted by capitalism in distress to defeat the democratic political foundations with which it could be successfully linked in its period of creative expansion'.[14] Since 'capitalism' was assumed to be right-wing, that theory guaranteed to fascism a position on the right of the spectrum; and by the mid-Thirties no other explanation was much to be heard.

Few intellectuals saw, or wanted to see, the deep resemblance and common ancestry of socialist and fascist thought. Yeats had been a William Morris socialist in the 1880s; Hulme's *Speculations*, something of a cult book of the literary Right in the years between the wars, ends with an attentive examination of Sorel, a revolutionary socialist admired by both Lenin and Mussolini, and praised by Hulme, who had translated him, as 'the most remarkable socialist since Marx' in reconciling revolutionary economics and classical ethics. Pound abused usury and finance-capital as roundly as any socialist, though always in a rhetoric perceptibly distinct.[15] Mussolini had been a revolutionary socialist until the First World War, and Hitler retained that title to the end of his days. Fascism and socialism alike had a horror of the market-place, of the 'cash-nexus' (as Carlyle had called it) supposedly at the heart of liberal democracy; both demanded massive powers for central authority, a single-party state and a purposive tyranny to replace the shifting near-chaos of the party system and competitive economics; both detested usury, or rent, or interest. Bernard Shaw, an avid Stalinist by the Thirties, publicly praised Mussolini and came close to praising Hitler as well, and openly rejoiced in the Italian conquest of Abyssinia.

Massive as the resemblances were, it was unfashionable to admit that they existed at all. The exceptions are individual, even eccentric. Wyndham Lewis perceived that National Socialism in Germany was indeed a version of socialism, a communism in uniform with a heady admixture of patriotism and marching-in-step: 'a copy – but not a "bourgeois" copy, rather a *military* copy – of Marxism.'[16] Oswald Mosley demanded fiercely radical measures in fiercely revolutionary rhetoric, and was to protest later, convincingly enough, that one cannot be a Fascist and a reactionary at the same time: 'A movement of the Right has nothing to do with fascism, which can be described as revolutionary but not as reactionary.'[17]

But this is not what literary intellectuals of the Thirties came to believe, to Right or to Left. The thrust of the literary Right was a fondness for decaying doctrines and values, a nostalgic conservatism.

★

In Britain, at least, the polarisation of Left and Right was late, and belongs to the mid-Thirties. Documents earlier than that do not naturally see socialism and fascism as opposites. The clarity or crudity of Left and Right was to come later; and the myth of fascism as a conservative force, being fundamentally a Marxist myth, had to wait to be heard until Marxism itself was widely accepted.

Meanwhile the professional definers of words were more cautious. In 1925 the Society for Pure English, in its cool, lexical way, observed of the new ruling dogma of Italy that in late nineteenth-century Sicily 'Socialist groups called "Fasci siciliani" became well known, through their riotous behaviour and revolutionary activities', and it outlined the rise of Mussolini from them down to the March on Rome in October 1922.[18] In the years before Hitler came to power it was not uncommon or especially tendentious to see Mussolini's Italy as an experiment in the 'Lenin–Trotsky school' of power, with elements of Sorel, syndicalism and guild socialism thrown in.[19] One early observer with no obvious axe to grind saw Nazism as part of a 'definite trend towards "Socialism", in the sense that Germans naturally expect the state to play a bigger part in their economic and cultural life than would ever be tolerated, for instance, in this country'.[20]

Left and Right are already common terms in the Britain of the early Thirties, but it is not yet unanimously clear that they correspond to socialism and fascism. D. H. Lawrence, in one of the last essays he ever wrote, speaks of Lenin and Mussolini as if they were distinct but by no means opposite cases, and as together illustrating the 'miracle, mystery and authority' that mankind will forever demand; 'Russia destroyed the Tsar to have Lenin and the present mechanical despotism, Italy has the rationalised despotism of Mussolini, and England is longing for a despot.'[21] Robert Graves, in his *Contemporary Techniques of Poetry* (1925), thought *The Waste Land* an outstanding instance of 'Left Wing verse',[22] though this is offered as political analogy, not as an account of Eliot's convictions; but Graves at that early date was ready to list Eliot, the Sitwells, Ford Madox Ford and Siegfried Sassoon as 'now definitely committed to revolution' in literary terms. An admiration for *The Waste Land,* for years after its first appearance, was felt to be appropriate to the young radical intelligence.

The only mention of Fascists in Roy Campbell's *Georgiad* (1931) – which at that date can only mean Italy – dismisses Fascist and socialist in a single blast as dour egalitarians, with little to choose between them. Five years later Campbell was to work and write for Franco; but here he abuses the Bloomsbury Fabians as spinsters and cissies

> whose collective dictatorial rule
> Would wake the devil in the tamest mule –
> For they're all members of the self-same school,
> And drilled, like Fascists, to enforce on all
> The standards of the middling and the small (p. 62).

Soon after 1933 all that would be brusquely revised, and not only by Campbell. Even the socialist origins of anti-semitism would be hastily forgotten, though in the Twenties they were scarcely even controversial. 'The struggle against Jewry', according to one Communist source, reporting Hitler's trial in Munich in 1924 after the failure of his putsch,

> has produced an anti-capitalistic spirit in the various ranks of Hitler's following . . .; after the failure of the Hitler putsch, a section of the former followers of the popular movement have expressed their support for the revolutionary proletariat and the Communist International.[23]

But ten years later everything was polarity. Resemblances and common origins were neglected. Men were unimpressed by the common élitism of the one-party state, since rival parties throughout Europe by then contested the title to a monopoly of power. Few men of letters perceived that state capitalism, being backed by the unheard-of powers of a totalitarian state, is the most brutal capitalism of all. The novelty of fascism did not by then render it objectionable to men of conservative instincts, as it deserved to do; it was enough that it was anti-Bolshevik. The antiquity of Marxism, a doctrine largely formed in the 1840s, was seldom thought to make it old hat, except to a few rare spirits who kept their heads and refused to be hurried or bullied. 'Out-of-date controversialising', Keynes called it bluntly in 1933, in a letter to Shaw, who had urged him to read Marx and Engels. Keynes refused to be impressed; they had 'invented a certain method of carrying on, and a vile manner of writing, both of which their successors have maintained with fidelity'.[24]

Such blasphemies against Marxist scripture were not much heeded. To be Marxist, on the whole, was felt to be up to date, bright-young-thing and *avant-garde*, and intelligent men convinced themselves by the hundreds that an early nineteenth-century German had solved the problems of industrial states a century later. When Hitler and Stalin became allies in August 1939, with the Molotov–Ribbentrop pact, and partitioned Poland weeks later, hardly any one saw these events as the reunion of a doctrine only recently sundered by the schisms of rival parties. The event was imagined to be an ideological monstrosity, or at the best an act of brutal necessity in the harsh game of international power politics. Oblivion had been as fast and as efficient as that.

★

The political hysteria of intellectuals in the Thirties has worn badly, and it is now difficult to see it as better than trivial. That can be true of the writers themselves, as they peer backwards towards their youth. Auden allowed the best of his Communist poems of the Thirties to be reprinted in an anthology in the 1960s only if accompanied by the following editorial note: 'Mr W. H. Auden considers these five poems to be trash which he is ashamed to have written.' [25] The poems he calls trash are 'Sir, No Man's Enemy', 'A Communist to Others', 'To a Writer on His Birthday', 'Spain' and 'September 1, 1939'. They had come to look trivial, by then; and yet they had represented a grim and dedicated triviality at the time, backed by big armies and mighty armaments. The intellectual debate of Left and Right was not shadow-boxing, least of all in Spain. It is simply that the dogmatic distance between the two sides, as in the religious wars of seventeenth-century Europe, has diminished with the lapse of time. The two teams had more convictions in common than they knew or cared to know.

That ignorance was in part wilful. No intelligent conservative can have admired Mussolini or Hitler without self-deception; and no radical with any will to see could doubt the deep conservatism, political and artistic, of Stalin's Russia, or the supreme capitalism of his total capitalism of state. Men believe what they will themselves to believe. It was a double triumph for collective hysteria. In the perfervid years of the Popular Front, with the pressures to conform that wars and rumours of wars can bring, it would be hard to set a term to the absurdities and contradictions that dedicated faith could sponsor.

6 | *The Myth of Catastrophe*

In September 1940 the Luftwaffe broke the air defences of London and set its docks on fire. Two Londoners, George Orwell and Cyril Connolly, watched the spectacle from a rooftop, 'struck by the size and beauty of the flames'. And as they watched, Connolly remarked: 'It's the end of capitalism. It's a judgement on us.'

'I didn't feel this to be so,' Orwell remarks in his diary, though he had already arrived at much the same conclusion on other grounds. A system was ending. 'The Stock Exchange will be pulled down,' and the wartime House of Commons was already no more than the shadowy Roman Senate in the age of the emperors.[1] It was only the aptness of one great fiery symbol that had failed to impress him.

A generation later, however, and Parliament, the monarchy and the Stock Exchange were still there; and hardly anybody, unless on the extreme fringes of political life, could find it natural to imagine that what had once been confidently abused as 'capitalism' could soon disappear. Even in Soviet, though not yet in Chinese Communist circles, that glib prophecy had ceased to be orthodox by the 1950s. The system lives that many thought must die. It was the catastrophic myth predicting its end which in the event was to prove mortal. It died in the Forties, drowned in a rhetoric of victory and the promise of a good world to come. I use the word 'myth', accordingly, in its familiar and dismissive sense, as of a story since discredited on later and better evidence. But the other word, 'catastrophe', needs to be seen in unusually neutral terms. It can be conceived of as a good. Some people, certainly, have wanted it; some have even wanted it ardently, and worked to make it happen.

Wanted or not, catastrophe is the master-myth of two literary generations, from D. H. Lawrence's *Rainbow* (1915) and *Women in Love* (1920), W. B. Yeats's 'Second Coming' (1920) and, two years

later, Joyce's *Ulysses* and Eliot's *The Waste Land*. It ends climactical-
ly, not with a whimper but a bang: with the Marxist apocalyptics of
W. H. Auden and others in the Thirties. That leaves an infinite
variety of motive and purpose; but the ultimate companionability of
many of these works was seen at the time, even by their own authors.
When T. S. Eliot reviewed *Ulysses* in the *Dial* in November 1923, he
hailed it warmly as a prose companion to his own poem, 'an im-
mense panorama of futility and anarchy' in modern life. Months
later, in the summer of 1924, Scott Fitzgerald wrote *The Great Gatsby*
in the intervals between reading Spengler on the decline of the
West.[2]

'Surely some revelation is at hand,' Yeats had just declared in his
'Second Coming', fearfully prophesying some nightmarish Messiah,
a 'rough beast, its hour come round at last'. Maynard Keynes, in the
opening pages of his *Economic Consequences of the Peace* (1919), had
already attacked the complacency of post-war England and talked
direfully of 'the fearful convulsions of a dying civilization' on the
Continent of Europe. In 1920, in *The Practice and Theory of Bolshevism*,
Bertrand Russell, though detesting Lenin and the new Soviet dictatorship he had just visited, bluntly called the Western economic
system 'doomed' and gave it, at the most, half a century to live; exactly half a century later he died himself, and the system had survived him. Ezra Pound, in his early cantos, abused a civilisation he
saw as built on usury, monopoly capital and empire. In the first
chapter of *Lady Chatterley's Lover*, written and twice rewritten in
Florence in 1926–8, Lawrence was soon unwittingly to echo a phrase
from the conclusion to *The Waste Land*, 'These fragments I have
shored against my ruins', though there is no evidence that he knew
the poem. In the third version of the novel, which was the first to
appear, he announced:

> The cataclysm has happened, we are among the ruins, we start to
> build up new little habitats, to have new little hopes. . . . We've
> got to live, no matter how many skies have fallen.

In the first version of the novel, a source-book more probable than
Eliot is hinted at: 'By the time the *Untergang des Abendlands* appeared,
Clifford was a smashed man'; wounded in France, he returned to
England paralysed from the waist down and sexually impotent, a
symbol of the condition of a people. The first part of Spengler's

Decline of the West had already begun to appear in German in 1918.

Such, then, was the nearly universal myth of literary intellectuals between the wars. Its form was notably divided by generation. For the older generation of the Twenties, catastrophe had already happened; and the West, as impotent as Clifford Chatterley, might as well be dead already. For the youthful optimists and utopians of the Thirties, by contrast, catastrophe was a doctrine of revolutionary faith, and the collapse of the old meant the triumph of the new. It is a shift from despair to iconoclastic hope. An illusion, in either event, since Western civilisation is still there.

★

Why did men so utterly various in conviction as Yeats, Lawrence, Joyce, Eliot, Bertrand Russell and the young Auden all believe that their civilisation was about to collapse? It is always a matter of arresting interest when highly intelligent men are mistaken in the same way, especially when they disagree about nearly everything else. One answer, though temptingly simple, would be merely evasive: that the myth was more or less answered by events themselves, that Hitler was Yeats's rough beast, and that the Blitz and the Holocaust were surely catastrophe enough for anyone. But the myth is too specific for that. Catastrophe is not merely disaster; it is something much more. It meant for all these men the total collapse of a civilisation and of the economic system that sustained it, and its replacement by another and totally contrasting civilisation. And we all know that in the West this has not happened.

More plausibly than that, one might argue that these men believed in catastrophe because something like it had already occurred: the horror of the trenches in 1914–18 and an unemployment which, from 1920 to the outbreak of war in 1939, scarcely ever in Great Britain dropped below the figure of one million. Add to all this the successive collapse of European democracies – Italy in October 1922 with the March on Rome, Germany in January 1933, and Spain after 1936 – and the catastrophic theme of literary Modernism, many would say, could be justified on simple descriptive grounds. Catastrophe had already happened, they would argue, or was happening; it was there as poets and novelists wrote. It had already occurred, in any case, decisively and to all appearances irreversibly, in Russia in October 1917. And the myth was not confined to men of letters. There were statesmen, too, who took an apocalyptic view: in February 1931 Sir Oswald Mosley left the Labour Party to found his New Party, which in the following year turned into the British Union of Fascists. It is often supposed, on accumulated evidence of this sort, that the doctrine of catastrophe between the wars was merely a natural response to what the eye saw and the ear heard. And in addition, there is now a reminder that the doctrine is a traditional one, that the 'powerful eschatological element in modern thought' is the most recent state of a long-standing cult; and that medieval and Renaissance Christians who believed in millenarian doctrines and the coming of Antichrist 'felt as we do'.[3]

The difficulties in both these arguments, the descriptive and the traditionalist, have never been adequately examined, and they are greater than has been observed. Let the second, on grounds of its enormous generality, be considered first: that modern Catastrophe derives from Judaeo–Christian Apocalypse. No one will deny that many intellectual convictions of the last hundred years and more, including those of Carlyle, Marx, Nietzsche, Max Nordau and Lawrence, have a harsh apocalyptic ring of a familiar and biblical kind. Not one of these men was a practising Jew or Christian, but again and again in their writings one smells the whiff of brimstone and hears the cry of the Damned and the chanting of the Blessed. Carlyle, in *Sartor Resartus* (1836), held that the 'old sick Society' of Europe should be 'deliberately burnt' as a creative act, 'in the faith that she is a Phoenix; and that a new heavenborn young one will rise out of her ashes'. Nordau, whose fame preceded Nietzsche's in the Britain of the Nineties, denounced Western civilisation in his *Degeneration* (1895) as a vast hospital of decadence and hysteria, a psychiatric ward for mystics, egomaniacs and self-indulged pessimists. Lawrence has often been seen as a strident latecomer in the long inexhaustible tradition of English Puritanism: a Puritan without Christianity, to be sure, but one whose diction reeks of chapel hymns and hellfire sermons. 'Except a seed die,' he wrote grimly to Bertrand Russell in May 1915, 'it bringeth not forth': and in his *Studies in Classic American Literature* (1923) he dubbed the sinking of the *Pequod* in *Moby Dick* as 'the doom of our white day'.[4] One title he considered early for *Women in Love* was *Dies Irae,* and his last book is called *Apocalypse* (1931). Fascism and communism, it could plausibly be argued, are formal political expressions of a similar certainty concerning a just and impending doom.

But all this does not explain, or even mention, the sheer uniqueness of twentieth-century apocalyptic despair. The tenth century A.D. may for all one knows offer some sort of parallel here, though by modern standards a woefully ill-documented one; but no age of Western literature has been obsessed by a myth of catastrophe as the early twentieth century, in its largely secular way, was obsessed by it. Other ages show instances of such obsession, but not the predominance of such instances. The line that stretches from *The Rainbow* through *Ulysses* and *The Waste Land* and *The Hollow Men* to the cry for worker-revolution in poems and tracts of the Thirties is unique in its continuity and intensity. It approaches unanimity. What writer or thinker of eminence in the Twenties and Thirties did not believe, fearfully or hopefully, that the known world was about to end? 'The old clock ticks on', wrote A. P. Herbert of capitalism, in his *Letter to the Electors of Oxford* in 1935. 'It is infinitely adaptable and has not, I think, exhausted its resources.' That was the extreme limit of reforming optimism, so far as one ebullient reformer could see, and Oxford University in 1935 responded by voting him into Parliament. But no more than that could be said: an old clock still ticked. It is the most cheerful gloss the Thirties could find to put on Eliot's cheerless conclusion about the coming end of the world, in *The Hollow Men*: 'not with a bang but a whimper'.

The problem of descriptive justification, which I posed first, is harder to unravel. It is not entirely clear what kind or quantity of historical evidence would satisfy anyone who still believes that those who wrote of catastrophe merely described what they knew. This is a dilemma of a familiar and even rewarding kind. Intellectual history conceals a host of unanswered, and sometimes unanswerable, questions in the logical form of the chicken-and-the-egg. Did men write of catastrophe because it was there, or was it there because men wrote of it? Were many Victorians optimistic because things were going well, or were things going well because they were optimists? A stock exchange is a very exact model of this aspect of intellectual history, and delicately illustrates the eternal reciprocity of thought and action. Does the market go up because clients are optimistic enough to buy; or are they optimistic because the market is in fact about to go up? In all these cases, there is a chain reaction of cause and effect where each effect, in its turn, becomes a cause. And as with stocks and shares, so with ideas: the original cause in thought or action may be forever undiscoverable, even while the chain of effects rewards the industry of the historical enquirer.

All that represents a difficulty to be posed, hardly a problem to be solved. But two warnings may be allowed. One is that in intellectual history, as in any other kind, a cause cannot follow its effect. If the myth of catastrophe, in its largely secular and twentieth-century form, existed in the minds of Nietzsche and Spengler before 1914, then it cannot have been caused by trench warfare or the Depression of 1931, though it may have been confirmed and enlarged by such events.

The other warning, equally commonplace as an abstraction, is in the form *post hoc ergo propter*. It is not safe in all instances to assume that the relations between ideas and events, or events and ideas, are causal at all. How can we know that the trenches or the Depression made men accept one or another version of an existent doctrine of catastrophe? Some would answer confidently that the hypothesis is so natural that it needs no proof, only the occasional confirmatory pat of documentary evidence. But this may be rash. *Ulysses* and *The Waste Land* were both written before the Depression; and if their pessimism was caused, even in part, by the First World War, why did they not speak of that war? *Ulysses* is set in the year 1904, when Joyce left Dublin forever; and *The Waste Land,* in those passages that verge on social realism, seems to be about the domestic trivialities of a peacetime London, though it mentions demobilisation and the 'hooded hordes' of Bolshevism. There is nothing impossible in the suggestion that Joyce and Eliot thought what they thought about Western civilisation before August 1914. Poets and novelists, after all, are under no obligation to write out of the present, or even out of the recent past; and a cause that looks obvious may prove on examination to be no cause at all.

By the Thirties, it is true, with its highly specific rhetoric of crisis, this dilemma of interpretation arises less often. The newspaper headlines are there in the works themselves; and the sense of imminent apocalypse is based, and explicitly based, on events as they occur. 'I see no way of stopping Fascism now', Kingsley Martin wrote in his diary in September 1934, more than a year after the Nazi accession to power in Germany. 'I give us one more year of National Government, then two or three years' more "Conservative–National" Government, then a short Labour Government, then Fascism. Seven more years to live! Very optimistic, because there will be street-fighting, etc. long before that.'[5] This is unusually specific, perhaps because it is private; but it creates a context in which to interpret other works of the Thirties. The first volume of Arnold Toynbee's *A Study of History* appeared in the same year, and announced the imminent collapse of the industrial–democratic states of the West. Its thesis evidently owes something to Spengler's *Untergang des Abendlandes* (1918–22), which Spengler had begun to write before the First World War; it was a book Lawrence had already referred to symbolically in his earlier versions of *Lady Chatterley's Lover*, which he wrote at a time when the English translation of Spengler (1926–9) was just appearing. Toynbee's title-page of 1934 bore three mottoes, all grim: the biblical 'Work while it is day'; the warning of Virgil's Sybil to Aeneas, 'Night is coming'; and, from the Anglo-Saxon poem 'The Battle of Maldon',

> Thought shall be the harder,
> Heart the keener,
> Mood shall be the more,
> As our might lessens.

Only doom was on offer, though some offered a utopia on the other side of doom. A new life might promise, but always and only across a sea of blood. W. H. Auden's *Dance of Death* (1933) begins with a voice announcing the prospect:

> We present to you this evening a picture of the decline of a class, of how its members dream of a new life, but secretly desire the old, for there is death inside them. We show you that death as a dancer.

The old bourgeoisie invite their imminent destruction; and when they are dead, history will declare them to have deserved extermination. These are words designed to provoke events, to make the Armageddon of class war happen, and quickly. 'What is begun', wrote Allen Hutt menacingly in *This Final Crisis* (1935), speaking of the coming proletarian revolution, 'will be carried out'. After that there will be no more crisis. By then the class enemy will have been extinguished.

It is tempting to answer that this, or something like it, is what happened after 1939. But did it? The first two years of world war saw Hitler and Stalin, those alleged class enemies, in open alliance; the remaining four showed Stalin in alliance with the capitalist West. On the orthodox Communist assumption that Moscow is the world spokesman for proletarian revolution, it is hard to see how these great events can be interpreted as a war between classes. And capitalism, as it is still sometimes called, has survived the London fires of September 1940; so have elective systems of government in the Western world; so have the 'decadent' forms of art they have traditionally tolerated, and so have the revolutionary critics they traditionally harbour, feed and heed. We are still here, one might answer the dead voices of the Thirties; and what is more, your successors are still free to preach at us, or against us, because we still let them.

A prophecy, admittedly, does not totally lose interest because events have proved it wrong. It joins a museum of discredited notions – to be taken out perhaps, some day, and redecorated, and even (in a new set of circumstances) proved to have been in some sense right, though right too soon. But none of this, if it ever happens, could rescue the highly immediate doom-predictions of the Thirties. In the advanced states of the Western world, neither Fascist nor Communist revolution happened within Kingsley Martin's limit of seven years, or for that matter within twenty-seven. As early as January 1943, George Orwell, that early-warning system for left-wing intellectuals, sounded a 'growing suspicion that we may all have underrated the strength of capitalism';[6] and the Labour electoral victory of April 1945, in an atmosphere of fading apocalypse, was rightly regarded by few, friend or foe, as heralding the end of the Stock Exchange. By then the talk was all of change, not of utopia: of reform, not of revolution. The doom prophets had fallen silent or joined the other side. 'The system', one pre-war socialist sadly remarked years later, when he had settled into the humdrum life of a Labour M.P., 'was stronger than we knew.'

★

How was the mistake made? It was a mistake committed by intellectuals and not, so far as guesswork, hearsay and recollection allow one to judge, by the generality of men. It is highly unlikely that most Englishmen or Frenchmen, still less Americans, believed between the wars that total catastrophe was imminent and inevitable, though many may have thought it among the range of possibilities. But intellectuals were different. 'These interwar writers', A. J. P. Taylor has remarked,

> present a puzzle to the historian. Literature, according to historical convention, reflects contemporary life and reveals its spirit. To judge from all leading writers, the barbarians were breaking in. The decline and fall of the Roman empire were being repeated. Civilized men could only lament and withdraw, as the writers did to their considerable profit. The writers were almost alone in feeling like this, and it is not easy to understand why they thus cut themselves off. By any more prosaic standard, this was the best time mankind, or at any rate Englishmen, had known. . . . It is hardly surprising that ordinary people found the great contemporary works of literature beyond them.[7]

The puzzle is even deeper when one reflects that Maynard Keynes, the most widely acclaimed economist of the age, was offering reasons for supposing the woes of the West might be remediable. Whether Keynes was right or wrong, on the evidence of subsequent history, in prescribing revisions for the Versailles treaty or for solving mass unemployment, are questions for others; what matters here is that an influential economic thinker, controversial in his views but always widely respected, should have argued that the situation was critical rather than hopeless. True, *The General Theory of Employment, Interest and Money* did not appear until January 1936, which is almost too late for this story. It is, in any case, not a book one can easily imagine in the hands of Yeats, Eliot or Auden. But Keynesian prescriptions for reform were available much earlier than this. The Liberal Yellow Book, written by a group of which he was a leading member, had appeared in 1928 as *Britain's Industrial Future*; and he had put what was most urgent in his case years earlier than that in pamphlets and articles. In an article in the *Nation*, for example, of 24 May 1924, 'Does Unemployment Need a Drastic Remedy?', he had proposed that the state should spend up to £100 millions a year on capital works at home, including the mass production of houses. Throughout his working life he thought talk of revolution mere claptrap, and old-fashioned claptrap at that; though he did not doubt that the hour was late, and that if governments did not act quickly a total collapse of the Western economic system was still possible. Keynesianism, then, was a doctrine of catastrophe-unless: the worst can still be avoided through swift and decisive political action by the existing instruments of government. But the task of avoiding catastrophe, as he often insisted, is not helped by a slavish intellectual dependence on nineteenth-century sources. In January 1935, just a year before *The General Theory* appeared, he wrote to Bernard Shaw that he had been rereading Marx and Engels and could still find in them 'nothing but out-of-date controversialising'; and he looked forward eagerly to *The General Theory*'s knocking away 'the Ricardian foundations of Marxism'. One of the established sources of the modern myth of catastrophe already seemed to him discredited both as a theory and as a matter of history.

All this, if accepted, would make the myth of catastrophe look antiquated as well as absurd. But then, in the Britain of the Thirties, it was not on the whole economists and political scientists who surrendered themselves uncritically to an admiration of Marxism or its Ricardian foundations. It was poets, dramatists and novelists. Why were they so little interested in Keynesian ideas of reform, or any other?

The answer, it seems clear, can only be in terms of deep ideological prejudice. They had made up their minds already: the situation, as early as 1931–2, was already judged to be beyond remedy. They had simply closed their minds to proposals for reform. History, that convenient scapegoat, had already in their view passed its final sentence on the modern age, and a reformer looked no better than a man rearranging deck chairs on the *Titanic*. There can be no turning back now, as Louis MacNeice explained in his verse dialogue of December 1933. 'An Eclogue for Christmas', and what must happen will happen:

> A. What will happen when the sniggering machine-guns in the
>   hands of the young men
>   Are trained on every flat and club and beauty parlour and
>   Father's den?
>   What will happen when our civilisation like a long-pent
>   balloon –
> B. What will happen will happen.

This is the Spenglerian prophecy of youthful gang rule that Scott Fitzgerald had read about in the summer when he was writing *The Great Gatsby,* and he believed in it to the end of his life: 'young people hungry for spoil', with 'the world as spoil'. In a letter of June 1940, written a week before the fall of France, he called Spengler's the 'dominant supercessive idea' of the coming age.[8] He must have been even more certain of that a week later, when a German army in France fulfilled a German prediction.

★

Why, and against the evidence of Keynes and others, was doom so convincing a hypothesis to literary intellectuals between the wars? Some familiar answers will begin to serve, though they will not serve altogether. There is the sheer intellectual prestige of pessimism; there is utopianism, that professional deformation of many a literary mind; there is an idealistic veneration for violence committed in the service of vast ideological causes; and there is a temperamental impatience with administrative half-measures that alleviate but do not cure. Many men, and especially many intellectuals, would rather be thought alarmist than complacent. Above and beyond all this, there is an overmastering contempt for merely practical and provisional considerations, and a love of dramatically opposed forces, a cops-and-robbers or cowboys-and-Indians view of political reality that dismisses gradualism precisely because it smudges the outlines of debate and diminishes the high drama of political contest to a mere indeterminacy. A struggle between between two contestants is always more satisfying to contemplate than one between three or more; and if it were proposed that the Oxford and Cambridge boat race should admit a third contender, it is easy to imagine the artistic outrage that the proposal would widely provoke. On dramatic grounds, two sides are best: capitalism or socialism, bourgeoisie or proletariat, Gentile or Jew. 'In our time', wrote Eliot in his preface to *After Strange Gods* (1934), 'controversy seems to me, on really fundamental matters, to be futile. . . . It requires common assumptions.' There was one deep chasm or divide, in the common view. It was between Left and Right, and no real debate across it was possible.

What is more, it is supremely satisfying to the aesthetic sense to watch a drama in which all the virtue is on one side. Such, after all, is the moral simplicity of melodrama and romance, and that simplicity underlies and supports the sophistications of Eliot's poetic technique, and proclaims itself unashamedly in the Marxist poets: 'Brothers, who when the sirens roar. . . .' It ultimately explains why remedial measures or policies of mend-and-make-do, which in practice govern so much of human affairs, and often so successfully, count for little or nothing in the apocalyptic consciousness. There is a deafness of the spirit. Much of the intellectual sophistications of the middle-aged Eliot or of the young Auden look much less sophisticated when one examines the ultimate loyalties they express. A sophistication of style can serve at times to mask a simplicity of content. Anything, for the partisan mind, is better than not having a side, just as anything is more endurable than the subtle kaleidoscope of party politics in a peaceful parliamentary state. In the brief interval before catastrophe, one may 'redeem the time' by faith or works; but the true way forward is to destroy and start anew. Even Hitler, being a revolutionary with the air of a martyr, could in some fashion look appealing. At least he knew what he wanted. 'Better an end with horror than a horror without end' is a remark of his that Orwell quotes with a rueful and qualified approval in a 1940 review of an unabridged version of *Mein Kampf*.[9] Life cannot just meander on. Intellectual nature abhors a vacuum; and if one apocalyptic vision is taken from mankind, like the Christian, then the same instinct will take to itself another. The catastrophe of revolution is just such a vision. 'Let them have eternal life', wrote Gide of the poor and oppressed, in his journal (7 August 1935), 'or give them revolution. Or rather', he corrected himself, 'take eternal life from them and you will have revolution.'

Events in the long run have served these prophesies ill. The West, at least, has been sent problems to solve and disasters to sustain rather than vast events of irreversible fatality. Catastrophe, in the end, was only a toy for intellectuals to play with, if one can conceive of a toy being put to such passionate uses. It was the subject of works of art, like religion in the High Renaissance; it was never a conclusion based on dispassionate enquiry or on the best use of recent and available evidence. History, in a word, has failed to present the intellectuals of the West with the tragic melodrama they earnestly asked of it. But then history, after all, is not a work of art. If it must be seen as one, in this century, then it may some day come to be regarded as a tragi-comedy: an action with tragic underplots and, for all we yet know, a happy ending.

7 | *The Politics of D. H. Lawrence*

Some writers survive less by what they assert than in the manner of their remembrance. D. H. Lawrence is a classic of the kind, and my concern here is not so much with what he believed as with what, somehow or other, he came to stand for, both to himself and to others. Always a myth-maker, like all great novelists, he was himself to grow into a myth, some of it of his own making. And that myth is fast bound with the fiction of his family origins; Lawrence was not above contributing to it directly, in his own last years; and since the Thirties it has accumulated, though embarrassed by occasional scholarly contradiction, into the proportions of a cult and the somnolence of a received idea.

Lawrence's own ideals of government belong in the European political tradition, if at all, to the pre-history of fascism. And yet no single term, not even proto-fascist, and certainly no party label, can do more than begin to describe what he believed. It cannot be seriously suggested that his alleged fascism ever had anything to do with a sustained support for any political party or movement, whether in or out of office. He died in March 1930, in any case, before that issue looked imperative to the British nation.

The claim that can be sensibly made here is twofold. First, he longed at times for a leader, even if no actual leader satisfied him, adopting after the outbreak of war in 1914 a taste for dictatorial over-assertion in his public writings and even in his letters. Bertrand Russell was to complain in his *Autobiography* that Lawrence used to tell him what he *must* preach 'in the language of a Fascist dictator', underlining the word 'must' thirteen times.[1] The epilogue to *Movements in European History* (1921), which Lawrence wrote soon after the First World War, calls on every youth, in ringing Nietzschean tones, to choose nobility for himself, and to 'follow only the leader who is a star of the new, *natural Noblesse*.[2] Second, his obsessions with 'blood-consciousness' or 'blood-knowing' was understandably to remind some of National Socialism in the years after his death. Russell claims to have rejected it, when he first heard it, as 'frankly rubbish', adding: 'though I did not then know that it led straight to Auschwitz'.[3] The verb 'to lead' is evidently incautious here. Events in central Europe would hardly have gone otherwise if Lawrence had never lived or written, and few have wished to argue that he created a tolerance for intellectual fascism among intellectuals at home. On the other hand, the fact of a doctrinal kinship remains: and Lawrence plainly viewed the coming national revival in Germany with a gloating expectation. Travelling up the Rhine, he wrote in 1928, you realise that 'something has happened to the human soul, beyond all help'. And that 'something' is primitive:

> The ancient spirit of prehistoric Germany coming back, at the end of history. . . . Something about the Germanic races is unalterable. White-skinned, elemental, and dangerous, . . . recoiling towards Tartary, the destructive vortex of Tartary. It is fate.

But a fate for which Britain is in part to blame: 'We have brought it about ourselves – by a Ruhr occupation, by an English nullity, and by a German false will'.[4]

It would be absurd to attribute much political influence to utterances of this sort. In the Thirties Lawrence was quoted more often, and more sympathetically, by writers of the Left than of the Right, though as feelings mounted high in the years of bitter polarity after 1936 it became clear he could satisfy neither party. He was not a member, if even an acquaintance, of that shortlived group of 1914 composed of Pound, Eliot and Wyndham Lewis; and Eliot, shortly after his death, was to stigmatise him in his Virginia lectures, *After Strange Gods* (1934), as one literary symptom among many of a perilous moral decay in Anglo-Saxon literary culture. No Marxist could approve him, though some could admire. And that isolation of fame poses the paradox in its sharpest form. He was widely held, by the later Thirties, to have been at once a regressive political advocate and a revered spokesman for working-class life. He was great without being good. But to unravel that paradox, the myth of Lawrence's working-class origins must be considered.

★

Lawrence, who was born in 1885, was the son of a contractor in a Nottinghamshire coalmine and of a former schoolmistress of some cultivation and social standing. The common assertion that his father was a miner, though not false, is misleading in context: he was not, by the period of Lawrence's upbringing, dependent on wages, being in charge of a group of miners, and his income was good. If his manners were rough, and at times even wild, this needs to be measured against the superior existence his wife created at Eastwood for the sons who, as she successfully resolved, would never work in a mine. Professor J. D. Chambers, the brother of Jessie Chambers and himself a social historian, has described Lawrence's world intimately, since he knew it in his youth, in a preface to the new edition (1965) of his sister's memoir *D. H. Lawrence: a Personal Record* (1935). It is untrue, he insists, that Lawrence's family lived in poverty; his father had been 'a highly skilled man, bringing home good money, occupying a house with a bay window and separate "entry" of which the Lawrences were immensely proud, and handing over to his wife enough money to give three of their five children a good education';[5] and he quotes a contemporary as recalling that 'though Mr. Lawrence went home merry, he was never drunk nor aggressive' – a recollection possibly selective or incomplete.

But events have since conspired to make Lawrence's childhood and youth seem grim with poverty. The mean terraced house marked as his birthplace, as all pilgrims to Eastwood should be told, ceased to be his home when he was six, and he lived in a superior residence on the hill above till he was eighteen. 'The Lawrences were moving up in the world', Chambers remarks of this move, 'and were very conscious of the fact.'[6] He was soon sent to Nottingham High School for the best schooling to be had locally, and after a few months as a clerk became a student at the University College there, to become a London schoolmaster in 1908 – achieving independence from his parents at the late age of twenty-three. Four years later he ran off with a German aristocrat, Frieda von Richthofen, the wife of his Nottingham professor. His early years presented opportunities for observing the lives of wage-earners rather than an experience of that life, and labourers are more often figures in the landscape of Lawrence's novels than principal actors there. Though his distrustful hatred of the Gentleman grew more bitter with age, he was as skilled as his friend E. M. Forster in portraying, and from within, the minds of young ladies of cultivated tastes; and the two intelligent sisters in *Women in Love* (1920) are as clear evidence for Lawrence's acquaintance with civilised gentility as the sisters in *Howards End* are for Forster's. On any ordinary interpretation of the evidence, untroubled by hearsay or prejudice, no one would readily call Lawrence's upbringing or early manhood working-class, though some of it was lived within sight and sound of collier life.

Lawrence's literary début occurred in November 1909, when Ford Madox Ford, then Hueffer, published some of his poems in the *English Review*. To the literary London into which Ford introduced him, Lawrence looked like a cheerful young Croydon schoolmaster from the Midlands. His personality does not seem to have been widely regarded as baseborn. Years later his headmaster recalled him as unrobust, his hands 'fragile, long fingered, expressive, well controlled', unpretentious in dress and gay and self-assured in manner: 'His expression always showed a kind of confident amusement. It was rarely serious.'[7] And Helen Corke remembers him in those years as 'polite and gay', with a passion for books, music and intellectual talk.[8] His background was admittedly distinctive, and he spoke with a Midlands accent he was to keep to the end of his days. But then literary London is well used to welcoming bright young sparks from the provinces to inform them about how life is lived south of the river, west of Hounslow and north of Potters Bar. It had recently opened its doors and its arms, after all, to H.G. Wells and Arnold Bennett. Lawrence's quick progress through that world, and through literary country houses like Lady Ottoline Morrell's Garsington, carries no hint of social exclusion. He later recalled how he had found London, as a young man, 'thrilling, thrilling, thrilling, the vast and roaring heart of all adventure'.[9] He was not – or certainly not in any continuous sense – a social failure in that world. Lady Cynthia Asquith, the Prime Minister's daughter-in-law, had the Lawrences to stay in 1915, and reported in her diaries without any hint of condescension that she found them 'the most intoxicating company in the world', and Lawrence's own talk 'extraordinarily real and living'.[10] If Bloomsbury found him excessively dogmatic at times, it does not seem to have jibbed at his social origins.

A number of obituaries in 1930, it is true, including E. M. Forster's, refer to him as of the working class, and without qualification;[11] but this is late evidence, the references are casual, and nothing is made of the matter. Virginia Woolf, a year or two after his death, was to confide to her diary that she found his novels 'airless, confined'; but it was his preaching she objected to, not his social vulgarity. By then Stephen Potter's *D. H. Lawrence: A First Study* (1930) had already appeared, proofread as its subject lay dying in the south of France, and Potter makes little or nothing of any issue of proletarian culture. Lawrence's typical readers in the Twenties, he believed, before his reputation declined late in the decade, were commonly 'youngish, normally educated, somewhat conventional men who, attracted by hearsay knowledge of Lawrence as a breaker-down of established things, have made use of him, or have naturally taken to him, as a means to make their own continued growth easier'.[12] A liberator of opinion, then, and especially of polite opinion; but no emphasis is laid on any humility of origin, only on iconoclasm, though his father is curtly described as a miner and his mother as 'superior', in inverted commas, and 'a lady'. It was the conventions he broke that disturbingly mattered, and his fabled interest in savages, animals and the Holy Ghost.

This seems equally the view of those who knew him personally. Richard Aldington, in a pamphlet that appeared in the year of Lawrence's death, reports on their conversations together as those of a lively if over-assertive sage in the English heretic tradition; and in 1931 John Middleton Murry, in his highly controversial *Son of Woman*, represented the Lawrence he had known as a victim of love consumed by its devouring fire, briefly mentioning his parentage as of 'a collier father and a bourgeoise mother'.[13] A few years later William Empson, in *Some Versions of Pastoral* (1935), declined to generalise: 'D. H. Lawrence's refusal to write proletarian literature was an important choice, but he was a complicated person'.[14] There was no widespread tendency, as early as that, to see Lawrence's own origins or the social subject-matter of his fiction as exceptional. Only his genius was that.

A myth, however, was shortly to form. The true original of Lawrence's reputation as a proletarian writer may have been his first literary sponsor, Ford Maddox Ford, who in an article in *American Mercury* (June 1936) written a few years before his own death blandly recalled his discovery of a new talent long before in 1909. The article, which was promptly collected in his *Portraits from Life* (1937), saw the young Lawrence as a social intruder into literary London, and the inventor of a new social class for English fiction. Ford wrote as if the industrial novel had never existed before in Victorian

England. Gissing, Wells, Bennett and Mark Rutherford, he argued, had already written about the 'lower middle classes'; but the 'completely different class of the artisan, the industrialist, and the unskilled labourer was completely unvoiced and unknown'. The article is a witty study in social embarrassment, remembered or misremembered over more than a quarter of a century: embarrassment at the prospect of being addressed as Sir by a miner's son in his editorial office; embarrassment at being so addressed; at hearing Lawrence speak so much of his own mother, whom Ford never met, and at actually meeting his father, who got drunk and had a good hand with mechanical tools. The fact seemed to him entirely symbolic of the young David's verbal artistry: 'It was probably not for nothing that the father of Jesus was a carpenter', Ford remarks pontifically. In his view Lawrence was not just a labouring-class novelist, but a novelist in whom the labouring virtues enriched a prose masterful with a sense of craft and form.

Marxist critics, meanwhile, were unimpressed. John Strachey in *The Coming Struggle for Power* (1932) and Christopher Caudwell in *Studies in a Dying Culture* (1938), which was written by 1936, make no heroic claims. Lawrence was a bourgeois artist, in their view; right, as Caudwell believed, in his perception that an artist must be a prophet, but 'ultimately Fascist and not Communist', though consistently nothing at all, and a prophet of 'regression, of neurosis, of the return to the primitive'.[15] George Orwell, by contrast, was more acquiescent, and *The Road to Wigan Pier* (1937) accepted him as a genuine proletarian who, like others from his class, had regrettably learned to know the ways of the middle class by the common but mistaken route of literary London.

By the late Thirties, though no earlier, Lawrence's status as a working-class novelist is beginning to be taken for granted, and by the Forties it is a commonplace. F. R. Leavis, in his 'Keynes, Lawrence and Cambridge' (1949), sided passionately with Lawrence over his meeting with Keynes and Russell in Cambridge in March 1915, and in the bluntest class terms: Lawrence, he believed, had been 'formed in a working class in which intellectual interests were bound up with the social life of home and chapel', not to mention breadwinning, all of which could only give him an 'enormous advantage in experience' over a mere Cambridge don.[16] Though Lawrence's early life had in fact been sheltered by an exceptionally protective mother, and his adult career utterly confined to schoolteaching and writing, he was by now achieving the enviable status of an existential hero, and without any of the physical exertions customarily required of that status. A Nietzschean rhetoric of life-affirmation (*Lebensbejahung*), which he had found in the Croydon Public Library of 1908–9, if not earlier, was belatedly to re-enter the bloodstream of English criticism in the *Scrutiny* of the 1940s, a strident vitalism fit to replace 'the dead materialism of Marx socialism and Soviets'[17] and the decay of the West. The dogma of a new aristocracy of energy and a 'revolution of life' was now heard in Cambridge classrooms, and soon elsewhere; and 'life' came to mean an imagined world beyond and behind the industrial revolution, a pastoral of English nature preserved, through an heroic act of will, by the very slaves of the machine.

By 1957, in Richard Hoggart's *The Uses of Literacy*, even Lawrence's mother had become working class: 'Notice that many old working-class women have a habitual gesture which illuminates the years of their life behind. D. H. Lawrence remarked it in his mother. . . .'[18] By the 1950s Lawrence's working-class origins amount to a standard intellectual-socialist myth. Raymond Williams, independently of Hoggart, represents the young Lawrence in his *Culture and Society 1780–1950* (1958) as struggling to escape 'his function of replacement' in the industrial working class, and later 'moving into the middle-class'.[19] And yet there is no real evidence that Lawrence was ever outside the middle class, as that phrase is most commonly understood, at any time in his life. By the Fifties, for all that, the proletarian myth had taken up its lodging in Academe.

★

Lawrence's standing as a working-class writer, though rarely accepted in his lifetime or even in the Thirties, is easier to understand if his own contribution is studied through his later years. His liberation from his mother's influence was plainly a slow process; it did not end with his elopement in 1912, but in some sense lasted all his life, so that it was only in his last years that he allowed himself in his own mind to take his father's side in the bitter parental struggle. There is a further possibility: that it was only in his last years that the humbler status of his father came to look disputatiously convenient. Men sometimes discover in their middle years that an origin they once found disadvantageous can be turned to an unlooked-for account. The social movement of Lawrence's fiction, with notable exceptions, is downwards, and the social predominance of servants, like Mellors in *Lady Chatterley's Lover*, is largely a characteristic of the middle-aged novelist of the Twenties. The young Lawrence, by all contemporary accounts – and they are both numerous and highly particular – was weakly and genteel, and that is decidedly the aura of his first novel, *The White Peacock* (1911). If the Cyril of that novel is not exactly the young Lawrence, he cannot be very far from what his mother had wished for him; and his closest acquaintances in the London of 1908–12, such as Helen Corke, were themselves in no doubt about the similarity.[20] But in his early forties – he died not yet forty-five – Lawrence appears, in some moods at least, to have adopted the mask of the labourer, or at least of one who has known hard labour at first hand. This was an impression he sometimes liked to give to superior acquaintances, perhaps as a defence against their superiority. Edith Sitwell, who visited the Lawrences in Tuscany in the late 1920s, recalled how determined he then seemed 'to impress upon us that he was a son of toil', how much he hated gentlemen, and how he tried to embarrass the Sitwells by adverting often to 'the contrast between his childhood and ours'.[21] That contrast is real enough, but the pose failed to impress them – perhaps because Frieda had proudly written her aristocratic maiden name, '*geborene* von Richthofen', in their visitor's book. 'Of course she was born!', Sir George Sitwell had exclaimed to them, in some puzzlement. 'Everybody is.'

In 'Red-Herring', a poem included in *Pansies* (1929), Lawrence calls himself an in-between, or one who by virtue of his mixed parentage is neither fish, flesh nor fowl – a claim palpably distinct from the claim to working-class status:

> My father was a working man,
>   and a collier was he . . .
> My mother was a superior soul,
>   a superior soul was she,
> Cut out to play a superior rôle
>   in the god-damn bourgeoisie.

In the 'Autobiographical Sketch' he wrote near the end of his life, he represented his father as 'a coal-miner, scarcely able to read or write', and his mother as 'from the bourgeoisie, the cultural element in the house', describing himself in hunted terms as belonging to a class apart in a 'purely bourgeois school' at Nottingham where he managed to make 'a couple of bourgeois friendships', though he 'instinctively recoiled away from the bourgeoisie', there and at the university, preferring 'the powerful life in a miner's kitchen' to the libraries and drawing-rooms of his 'proper bourgeois aunts'.[22] The resoundingly alien word 'bourgeois' rings doubly false here: false to the facts of his life, and false to his language. This is not the speech of the miner's kitchen or of an Edwardian Croydon schoolteacher. 'Bourgeois' is a Frieda-word, one may suspect; it is part of the novelist's mask. 'No writer is more conscious of class distinctions than Lawrence', as Eliot percipiently observed in a parenthesis in his Virginia lectures. But the consciousness here is a false one; and it is above all unsubtle. And English class distinctions call for subtlety, if anything does; for all the subtlety that Lawrence, on other occasions, abundantly possessed, and even something more.

But then Lawrence's grasp of English social realities after 1918 was often felt to be a fading one. He scarcely lived in England after the war, and Aldington was to remark of his conversation that 'in some respects Lawrence never got beyond 1912, and at odd times startles one by some echo of London life in those distant days'.[23] This is an aspect of his fiction still too little explored. Its social resonances stop, it could be argued, at about the time of his flight to the Continent in 1912. Though he was to return to England after that time, he was to live only rootlessly there; and most of his life after 1918 was to be spend in a series of resorts, in every sense of the word: Taormina in Sicily, an Australian beach house, New Mexico, Old Mexico, Florence and the south of France. As his conceptual life of mind advanced, even raced, his experienced life, and even his grasp on recollected experience, dwindled and withered away. The agony of his last return to Eastwood, which he described himself, has been even more vividly recalled by the friend who accompanied him there in 1926. Lawrence's face was contorted with pain, he averted his eyes from his old home, and bitterly refused ever again to return: 'Never! I hate the damned place.'[24] He was the most rootless of uprooted men, with little more to stare at than landscapes and the faces of other expatriates, and with a diminishing capacity to listen.

Meanwhile a remembered intellectual life drawn from the England of his early manhood aged in his mind, growing at once more dogmatic and less firmly related to any world he could see or touch. In some ways he seemed a very old-fashioned writer by the later Twenties. Ford remarked that when he settled in London, in 1908, he was influenced by a set who, in 'inverted puritanism', had insisted on 'nebulously glooming about sex', and added that when the manuscript of *The Trespasser* (1912) first reached him, in an early and uncompleted form, it reminded him of 'a schoolboy larking among placket holes, dialoguing with a Wesleyan minister who had been converted to Ibsen'. Those walks on the Surrey hills with Helen Corke, on whose diary the novel is based, and the world of passionate mental self-improvement that obsessed his early manhood, count for far more in his writings than any miner's kitchen. Helen Corke, in her autobiography, speaks of his passion then for Swinburne, and his reading of Wells, Bennett, Forster and Walter de la Mare. But even before he left Eastwood, library books had 'flowed through the house', according to J. D. Chambers, 'and floods of talk about their authors: Hardy, Bennett, Wells, Shaw, Huxley, Darwin, Conrad', as well as such foreign authors as Anatole France, Dostoevsky, Tolstoy, Turgenev, Schopenhauer 'and I think Nietzsche', along with Palgrave's *Golden Treasury*.[25] Lawrence was a formidably well-read twenty-three-year-old when he left home for the metropolis, and in the most fashionable modern authors, both British and Continental. No wonder he was not thought of as inferior in literary London. He was not inferior.

To the world that followed the peace of 1918, however, he came to look more like an impressive or embarrassing remnant of a dated Edwardian radicalism. His social world had inevitably ceased to exist, much as Forster's had. His world of ideas had fared no better. As an exile he seems to have been fired by a blind instinct for retribution against a homeland where he had succeeded so fast and so easily, and where he had ceased as fast to be a fashion. Such a man must have needed myths, and the myth of a lowly birth and harsh upbringing may have been a consolation. He believed in it himself, by his last years; he believed it before the world itself ever did. And years after his death the literary world, or that part of it that is able to preserve a sufficient indifference to sources, decided to trust the teller rather than the tale, and came to believe it too.

8 | Race and the Socialists

The racial interests of early socialist thinkers have already been scrutinised by historians; and it now seems less paradoxical than once it did to contemplate the post-war emigration policies of the Soviet Union, the fervent anti-semitism of Black Panthers in the United States, or the electoral collaboration in Great Britain in the 1970s between Mr. Enoch Powell and the Labour Party. For that matter, it is no longer easy to be confident that Hitler's title for his National Socialist movement was either hypocritical or inaccurate.

But existing studies[1] of the subject suffer from several limitations, which I list here mainly in the hope of escaping them.

First, they have almost always assumed that racial theories are absurd, even criminally absurd, so that they have usually been exercises in moral indignation as much as scholarly enquiries.

Second, they have usually supposed that 'race' and its compounds, for the Victorians, meant much what it means for the twentieth century. This has led to conceptual muddles and to misinterpretations of nineteenth-century texts.[2]

Third, they have emphasised Jewry almost to the exclusion of other issues.

And fourth, they have concentrated on France and Germany, including those German expatriates Marx and Engels. I shall concentrate here on Britain, including Marx and Engels as immigrants.

As for the alleged criminal absurdity of racialism, this is a question where neutrality can be found easy, indeed almost unavoidable, especially when it is based on a genuine and total agnosticism. I simply do not know, or know of any way of ascertaining, whether one race is superior to another. Consider, as an instance, the impressively vexed question of the relative intelligence of blacks and whites. If experts could one day devise intelligence tests that were widely accepted as accurate, and were to examine a wide sample of both races living in broadly similar educational circumstances in, say, Detroit or Wolverhampton; then I do not know, and cannot even guess, whether the resulting averages of intelligence would be similar or not. That is what neutrality and agnosticism mean here. If positive conclusions in this form are what racialism is about, then the existing evidence does not clearly encourage either racialism or anti-racialism; and this neutrality, accompanied as it should be by an analytical coolness, may present argumentative advantages. Not that anyone is under any obligation to be cool all the time. The neutral is in no way bound to deny himself the indignation of any decent man when confronted with instances of racialist or anti-racialist intolerance – whether in the field of immigration policy, for instance, or in the refusal of an experimental scientist to consider evidence that might prove politically unpalatable.

The conceptual muddles that afflict the subject, historically considered, are more complicated, and they call for a more extended analysis. The problem is at once lexical and logical. As a lexical matter, 'racialism' and 'racialist' are not recorded in English in the nineteenth century. The *Oxford English Dictionary* in its Supplement gives 'racialism' first in 1907, and 'racialist' only in 1930. ('Racial', on the other hand, is recorded as early as 1862.) 'Racism' and 'racist' are fairly recent American formations which are essentially synonymous, and British usage may still choose to assimilate them or not.

The logical problem is twofold. First, it would not have been a necessary assumption in Victorian debate, as it has commonly been since the 1930s, to suppose that an interest in racial differences involves a conviction in favour of the superiority of one's own. One might hold racial views, as more than one Victorian intellectual did, which maintained the superiority of another race – if not a total superiority, then on that operated at least in some vital respect. George Eliot's admiration for the Jews, and Matthew Arnold's for the Celts, are instances of what I have called bright as opposed to dark racial theory.[3] Other races have something to teach us, in this view. But nobody in the twentieth century seems to use racialism to mean this; as a matter of ordinary observation, the word nowadays can only refer to a doctrine that sees other races as inferior to one's won.

The second logical problem lies in the contrast between the genetic and the cultural. An interest in race since the 1930s has commonly meant a version of genetic theory concerning such hereditable strengths and weaknesses as intelligence or stupidity, physical prowess or its absence. This is a possible Victorian usage, but not the commonest. The commonest Victorian sense of 'race' and its compounds refers to a community of culture, where community can mean a unit as small as the family or as large as an empire, and where culture can refer to a language, an artistic inheritance, a religion, or any combination of these. Tennyson uses the word in all these senses: here is an instance, from *In Memoriam* (1850), of the most confined of all senses, to mean a family:

> As sometimes in a dead man's face,
>   To those that watch it more and more,
>   A likeness hardly seen before
> Comes out – to some one of his race.   (lxxiii)

Winston Churchill, who was born in 1874, was perhaps the last British statesman to use the word in its Victorian sense of a cultural community, and he continued to do so until his retirement from public life in the 1960s: his last book, an abridgement of his *History of the English-Speaking Peoples,* appeared some months before his death as *The Island Race* (1964). The cultural use of the word was the predominant use in Victorian English.

It was also the most richly charged. The supreme difficulty for the twentieth-century mind in encountering that of the nineteenth in this matter is to understand that, to many or most Victorians, contempt for the cultural attributes of race was likely to be more hurtful, and harder to forgive, than contempt for genetic composition. This shift of emphasis was to have curious consequences. It was the movement of interest towards the genetic in the Thirties and Forties that left old-fashioned anti-semites like T. S. Eliot in so embarrassed a position; they had embraced a view before the First World War which, after 1933, they were forced to contemplate in the light of events they had neither willed nor predicted. 'The worst thing about Hitler', a friend of Eliot's once remarked, 'was that he made an *intelligent* anti-semitism impossible for a generation.' Victorian views about other races, when hostile or critical, are more often like Eliot's than Hitler's. They criticise the cultural values of another community.

Such criticism was not felt to be any less devastating than genetic criticism. On the contrary, many Victorians would have thought genetic theories like Robert Knox's in *The Races of Men* (1850), or Sir Francis Galton's views about hereditary talent within families, as remotely bookish and scarcely hurtful to anyone. What the London Ethnological Society deliberated at its meetings was of very distant concern to ordinary Victorians, and even to most Victorian intellectuals. Knox's and Galton's were scientific speculations, not assertions about life as it is lived. It was only when you attacked the religious and ethical assumptions of a minority in your midst that you began to give offence. The cultural charge was ordinarily more offensive than the genetic. Consider Dickens's letter of 10 July 1863 to a Jewish lady, Mrs Eliza Davis, who had complained to him about the character of Fagin. This is Dickens's defence:

> Fagin in *Oliver Twist* is a Jew, because it unfortunately was true, of the time to which that story refers, that that class of criminal almost invariably *was* a Jew. But surely no sensible man or woman of your persuasion can fail to observe – firstly, that all the rest of the wicked *dramatis personae* are Christians; and secondly, that he is called 'The Jew' not because of his religion, but because of his race. If I were ever to write a story in which I pursued a Frenchman or a Spaniard as 'the Roman Catholic', I should do a very indecent and unjustifiable thing. . .

and he adds that to call Fagin a Jew is no worse than calling somebody else the 'Chinese'. Mrs Davis replied, warmly if not persuasively, that 'the Jewish race and religion are inseparable'. A year later Dickens made amends by creating Riah, the kind, submissive old Jew of *Our Mutual Friend* (1864–5). In 1867–8, towards the end of his life and thirty years after the composition of *Oliver Twist*, he revised the novel, deleting numerous references to the 'the Jew' and replacing them with 'Fagin' or 'he'.

Dickens lived and wrote as a radical Liberal, even if his views on particular issues were not always either radical or liberal.[4] But in all this he did not stand alone. Trollope, who once described himself as an 'advanced conservative liberal', would have shared some of his assumptions on the question of race; and popular novelists like these are much more likely to establish a sense of what most men believed than scientists or pseudo-scientists like Galton or Knox. In Trollope's *The Way We Live Now* (1875), for example, Miss Georgiana Longstaffe, who is nearing thirty and desperate to marry, betrothes herself to a rich Jewish widower called Mr Brehgert:

> a fat, greasy man, good-looking in a certain degree, about fifty, with hair dyed black, and beard and moustache dyed a dark purple colour. The charm of his face consisted in a pair of very bright black eyes, which were, however, set too near together in his face for the general delight of Christians. (ch. 60)

But the real trouble about him, for Georgiana's old friend Lady Monogram, lay not so much in his physical characteristics as in his religion:

> The man was absolutely a Jew; – not a Jew that had been, as to whom there might possibly be a doubt whether he or his father or his grandfather had been the last Jew of the family; but a Jew that was.

And Lady Monogram counts up on her fingers the number of 'decent people' who had recently married Jews or Jewesses, as one concerned only with what the world thought of such matters:

> She was herself above all personal prejudices of that kind. Jew, Turk or infidel was nothing to her. She had seen enough of the world to be aware that her happiness did not lie in that direction, and could not depend in the least on the religion of her husband.

So religion counts socially for more, much more, than descent; and a conversion to Christianity, if only as a matter of form, sets most difficulties to rights. It was not what a Jew or a Chinese *is* that mainly concerned Dickens, or Trollope, or many of their readers – 'is' as an irreversible fact of birth – but rather the cultural environment that has formed them. Nurture is stronger than nature, in this view, and conversion an acceptable corrective. The admission of Jews to the House of Commons in 1858, when they were finally allowed to swear their own amended form of the oath, is an instance of this.[5] The immigration policy of the State of Israel is another: it offers free entry to anyone of the Jewish religion, or whose mother was of that religion, or whose mother's mother was. By contrast, the enthusiast for genetic theory, such as a National Socialist, is unimpressed by religious adherence. A Jew in Nazi-occupied Europe might in practice save himself by turning Christian or pretending to do so, but only to escape detection. In the last resort his religion was an irrelevance.

★

It might be considered tempting, in view of this distinction, to speak of cultural racialism and genetic racialism. I shall try to resist this temptation. Since 'racialism' is a twentieth-century word, and has long since come to apply only to genetic theories concerning the superiority of one race over another, it would be merely precious to imagine that it could refer to anything else. To call anyone a racialist, now and in the predictable future, could only mean to attribute to him superior views about his own genetically hereditable characteristics.

On the other hand, this usage must be admitted to leave two gaps in our descriptive instruments. The first matters little enough: but we now have no way, or at least no brief way, of describing someone who thinks another race superior to his own. That state of mind is doubtless too rare in twentieth-century polemics to cause much embarrassment. But the other gap is more serious. How are we to describe the view, common to many Victorians and still familiar, that *cultural* communities are as such subject to praise or blame? It is hard here not to coin a neologism – culturalism, perhaps – on the analogy of racialism. The word might be used to describe Dickens, Trollope, George Eliot, Matthew Arnold, T. S. Eliot and many before or since – not to mention the State of Israel and some of the Arab states that surround it. And the word is at least neutral enough, by virtue of its novelty, to excite no passions and to denote a highly important intellectual interest active in the literary consciousness of Europe at least since the Waverley novels.

Racialist and culturalist ideas are easily compatible, and often coexist. But the failure of modern historians to distinguish them has deformed our understanding of the question and misinterpreted much of the evidence. Many historians have started from a preconception that racialism was a common, even a universal assumption among educated Victorians. This is simply untrue, if the word is to be understood as it is now understood. There is no clear evidence that Melbourne, Gladstone, John Stuart Mill or Balfour publicly held racialist views – or privately either, so far as that assertion can mean anything. Some thought such views dangerous. Lord Acton, in private notes for his unwritten 'History of Liberty', named the theory of race as one of the four elements in 'the increasing denial of liberty' that he sensed around him in the 1870s and after; the others were theories of progress, Providence and perfectibility. And when Salisbury, in a facetious address as Prime Minister in Edinburgh in 1888, indiscreetly referred to an Indian parliamentary candidate as 'a black man' – adding, amid more Tory laughter, that he imagined 'the colour is not exactly black' – the Liberal Opposition mounted a public campaign for their candidate, and Gladstone demanded an apology.[6] Indeed it would not be easy to think of any Victorian statesman, apart from Disraeli, who avowed racialist views; and in Disraeli such views are more strongly an element of his fiction, notably in the Coningsby trilogy of 1844, 1845, 1847, than of his parliamentary utterances.

With men of letters, it is true, the list of racialists grows a little longer. But not much. Carlyle announced his contempt for the negro in his 'Occasional Discourse on the Nigger Question', an article that appeared in *Fraser's Magazine* in December 1849 as a contribution to the abolition debate; Mill was to reply in strenuously anti-racialist terms in the following month. T. H. Huxley, in an article on 'Emancipation – Black and White' that appeared in the *Reader* in May 1865, at the end of the American Civil War, argued for the racial inferiority of the negro, since the white man is 'bigger-brained and smaller-jawed'; but he thought all this an argument in favour of the emancipation of slaves, in his vigorously paradoxical way, since it meant that the masters had little or nothing to fear from equal competition. Dickens reacted emotionally to the Jamaica uprising of 1865 and its suppression, and on the side of Governor Eyre – though not in terms that make it altogether clear whether genetic considerations were paramount; and Carlyle joined in with him, sentimentally anti-sentimental as ever. Ruskin, a socialist, held that the upper classes were literally better bred than the lower, and in *Modern Painters* (pt IX, 1860) he urged a return of the concept of the gentleman to its 'primal, literal and perpetual meaning' as 'a man of pure race' (ch. 7).

A few years later Francis Galton's *Hereditary Genius* (1869) appeared, a statistical study of the connections between ability and family descent, examining the heredity of statesmen, men of letters, painters, oarsmen and North Country wrestlers. Galton, a close student of his cousin Charles Darwin's law of natural selection, saw races as the sum of individuals and families, each one fitted for the conditions of its existence by a long Darwinian process; and he rejected Spartan methods of breeding as 'alien and repulsive to modern feelings', though he favoured social policies designed to delay the marriage of the weak and to hasten that of the vigorous. But 'eugenics', a word Galton later invented, is largely neutral in this argument: it permits rather than requires racialism. By the twentieth century, outside the dreams of a few fanatics, it amounts to little more than a playful interest in the gossip of consanguinity. G. K. Chesterton, in his *Eugenics and other Evils* (1922), ironically offered H. G. Wells a medal 'as the Eugenist who destroyed Eugenics' in his *Mankind in the Making* (1903) by confessing that scientists no longer claimed an ability to predict with confidence the talents of the offspring. Interest was falling away. Maynard Keynes, in 'The Great Villiers Connection' (1928),[7] conceded 'a certain persistent element' in the talents of families, but the tone of his argument is amused. Eugenics had never laid much claim to conclusiveness, in its more distinguished exponents. By the early years of the twentieth century it looked little better than a minor Victorian hobbyhorse.

Carlyle, Disraeli, Huxley, Ruskin. . . . This does not exhaust the list of possible racialists among Victorian men of letters, and a combing of popular and boys' fiction might produce significantly more. But when all is said, it still fails to produce the result that some historians nowadays take for granted, or as proven: that racialism was a common or universal sentiment in Victorian Britain. The literary and documentary evidence against that assertion is overwhelming.

★

The case of Marx is a tangled one. The essay to which most historians first turn to study his views of race – 'On the Jewish Question', written several years before he settled in London – is not in the strictest sense an essay about a racial group. It first appeared in the *Deutsch–Französische Jahrbücher* in February 1844, and its title alone guarantees it a certain prominence in this debate. But its argument, which is abusively anti-Jewish, concerns the infiltration of 'Judenthum', or the spirit of Jewish commercialism, into Christendom, and the urgent need to extirpate it as a way of life. A culturalist argument, in short; and Marx appears to have gone on believing in it: it reappears in volume 1 of *Das Kapital* (1867), where Gentile capitalists are abused as 'inwardly circumcised Jews' (ch. 4, 1), absorbed into the usurious ethic of Judaism. All this has excited some natural indignation; but it is still unhelpful to confuse race with culture, or to suggest on the evidence of this essay that Marx's 'solution of the Jewish question was not very different from Adolf Hitler's'.[8] True, Marx did believe in extermination, and often boasted of that belief. The class war he promised was not a metaphor. 'We are ruthless', he wrote defiantly in the last number of the *Neue Rheinische Zeitung* in May 1849, addressing the governments of Germany, 'and ask no quarter from you. When our turn comes, we shall not disguise our terrorism. . . .' But evidence of racial (as opposed to social) extermination is not clearly present in the 1844 essay on the Jewish question. It does, however, exist.

Marx's attack on the Jews was essentially an attack on big finance – on a sect that had fattened itself on modern capitalism, converted Europe to its own moneygrubbing ethos, and backed every despot that asked for money, including the Russian Tsar in his war in the Crimea.

> Thus we find every tyrant backed by a Jew, as is every Pope by a Jesuit. In truth, the cravings of oppressors would be hopeless, and the practicability of war out of the question, if there were not an army of Jesuits to smother thought and a handful of Jews to ransack pockets.[9]

This exceeds anything in Engels, who thought anti-semitism the sign of a backward civilisation; though he too was capable of using the word 'Jew' as a term of abuse. On the other hand, it is only doubtfully a racialist assertion, since 'Jew' in this passage of Marx's, and in many similar passages, refers only to members of a religion. But the famous letter to Engels of July 1862, attacking Lassalle as '*niggerhaft*' in his physical characteristics, 'as the shape of his head and the growth of his hair indicates', can only be read as racialist abuse. Bebel and Bernstein, the first editors of the Marx–Engels correspondence, nervously deleted anti-Jewish references, and the Marxist faithful have sometimes felt obliged to deny the authenticity of this letter, though it now appears in the official East Berlin edition of the works of Marx and Engels.[10] Moreover, no earlier use of *niggerhaft* in German has yet been found,[11] so that Marx may be tentatively credited with the invention, or rather the adaptation from Anglo-American, of a key term of racial abuse into the German language.

It is sometimes suggested that this letter is merely a momentary expression of personal exasperation. But Marx and Engels, years before 1862, had already publicly supported a programme of racial extermination. In two articles probably written by Engels, and published by Marx in his *Neue Rheinische Zeitung* in January– February 1849, a programme had been announced for the Slavs of Eastern Europe. In these articles on Hungary and Panslavism, and on Democratic Panslavism, the struggle of the smaller Slav peoples against Habsburgian domination is represented as a reactionary movement against the more advanced forces of Europe in favour of the reactionary power of the Tsars. The argument here is openly ethnic, and only Germans, Poles and Magyars are given any credit as 'the bearers of progress'. The rest must go: 'The chief mission of all other races and peoples – large and small – is to perish in the revolutionary holocaust. Therefore they are counter-revolutionary.' This is because the Slavs, being backward, have failed to pursue the essential historical evolution of developing a bourgeoisie. All European countries contain 'left-overs of earlier inhabitants', now rightly brought into subjection by more advanced peoples:

> This ethnic trash always becomes and remains, until its complete extermination or loss of national status [*Vertilgung oder Ent-nationalisirung*], the most fanatic bearer of counter-revolution, because its entire existence is nothing more than protest against a great historical revolution.[12]

Among such waste products and 'ethnic trash' (*Völkerabfall*) Engels instances Scottish Jacobites, Bretons and Basques and especially, in his own time, the South Slavs whose aspirations could only bring Russian power deep into Europe. And the final article concludes: 'The next world war will cause not only reactionary classes and dynasties but also entire reactionary peoples to disappear from the earth. And that too is progress.'

This vision of historical progress linked to racial purification was not a brief interest of the Victorian socialists. As Marx and Engels aged, and as the prospect of instant revolution in the industrial states receded, their studies grew increasingly anthropological and prehistorical. Social Darwinism and an interest in eugenics had joined to suggest that progress was interpretable in racial terms. Marx's late notes on this subject – scribbled in his last, sad years of failure and illness in 1879–82 and used by Engels, after Marx's death in 1883, for his own researches into the history of family institutions – have only recently been made public, edited from the manuscripts in an Amsterdam library.[13] The macaronic jottings of an ageing revolutionary, copying and commenting in German and English on the writings of contemporary anthropologists such as L. H. Morgan and Sir Henry Maine, do not make for inviting perusal, and few will be found to read them through. But they help to establish that socialist and racialist convictions in that age were often complementary. Marx, Engels and other Victorian socialists were not socialists who also happened to be racialists, or racialists who happened also to be socialists. They openly believed that the one interest required the other. The connection has since been lost sight of, even obscured, and it needs to be explained.

Soon after the appearance of Darwin's *Origin of Species* in 1859, a book Marx seems to have read at once, he wrote to Lassalle that it provided the outline of an anthropological explanation of modern industrial societies, 'the scientific foundation of the historical class-war'.[14] The triumphant classes, which are the bearers of progress and emerge with the industrial revolution, are first the dominant bourgeoisie, and soon after a revolutionary proletariat. Marxian revolution is seen as the final stage of an accelerating historical process to be measured by thousands of years. In the heat of immediate revolutionary hopes, in the 1840s and 1850s, it was the final stage that naturally absorbed interest and energy. In Marx's last years, in the face of a realisation that revolution could not come in his own lifetime, the time-scale widened backwards as well as forwards. The evolution of human history was seen in vaster terms, with variations representing inferior stocks, suppressed, and still to be suppressed, by a process Darwinianly selective.[15] And the eventual triumph of communism, however delayed, would represent a return on a higher plane to the communism of property that had once prevailed in primitive families. Private property had only arisen at all under the pressure of procuring subsistence;[16] it remained small among savages, but grew suddenly vast under modern industrial conditions, with the result that the new industrial classes must inevitably go to war with each other over the power that it confers. No detail is too small or too tedious for Marx's interest, in these last years, in problems of kinship, tribal marriage customs and property rights among Red Indians, Australian aborigines, ancient Romans and modern Indians. But a connection between race and *Volk* emerges, and Maine is abused as a 'blockheaded Englishman' because he begins his analysis not with the *gens* but with its patriarch or chief, fails to notice that in primitive societies property is tribal or communal, not personal,[17] and that the evolution of products into commodities arises not from members of the same tribe but out of exchanges between tribes – a detail later incorporated by Engels into the 1894 edition of *Das Kapital*.[18]

If the difference between one people and another is seen, in prehistory at least, as a source of evolutionary progress, then the early articles on Panslavism and their condemnation of historical left-overs like Highlanders, Bretons and Basques can be seen as completing this racial analysis in a contemporary context. Equality may be pursued – may have to be pursued – by killing those who are genetically unequal. Even in modern industrial societies, history has left socialists a variety of little mopping-up tasks to perform. An ancient process of natural selection will need to be completed by a proletarian dictatorship, once it has seized power through revolutionary terror.

Socialist racialism, then, is already present in published records in the nineteenth century, but grows much clearer in its outline when related to materials only recently published or collected for the first time. Set these materials beside the writings of native-born Victorian socialists such as Ruskin, Havelock Ellis, Beatrice Webb and H. G. Wells, and certain long-standing puzzles about their attitude to Jews and other races may be soluble. It has sometimes been supposed, for instance, that slighting remarks in their writings on other communities are merely cultural in their emphasis; or merely instances of what many Victorian intellectuals accepted regardless of their politics. Neither explanation will now do.

Beatrice Webb's concern about the sweat-shops of East London in the 1880s, many of them run by Polish-Jewish immigrants, could be mistaken for resentment against immigrants rather than hatred of a racial type. But a remark in her autobiography, *My Apprenticeship* (1926), makes this less likely. Believing herself to be of remotely Jewish origin, she conceived of having noticed in East End Jews a quality which she might herself have inherited genetically: 'It was the "overcoming by yielding" type of will, inherited from my father, which, when I was living amid the Jews in East London, I thought I recognised as a racial characteristic.'[19] In an article in the *New Statesman* (30 August 1913) she and her husband Sidney Webb had already warned against a future cataclysm that might destroy the civilisation of 'the Western European races' in favour of 'the negro, the Kaffir, or the Chinese' – a possibility the Webbs viewed as a 'melancholy conclusion'.

Havelock Ellis, at the same time, put the positive side of the case. Socialism would require the purification of the racial stock of mankind. In *The Task of Social Hygiene* (1912) he wrote:

> The question of breed, the production of fine individuals, the elevation of the ideal of quality in human production over that of mere quantity, begins to be seen not merely as a noble ideal in itself, but as the only method by which Socialism can be enabled to continue on its present path.[20]

The idea could have immediate and practical consequences. H. G. Wells, in *Anticipations* (1902), made in the bluntest terms a case for socialist extermination in the cause of racial fitness. Those 'swarms of black, and brown, and dirty-white, and yellow people, who do not come into the new needs of efficiency' will simply have to go: 'The world is a world, not a charitable institution, and I take it they will have to go. The whole tenor and meaning of the world, as I see it, is that they have to go.'[21]

The euphemism Wells employs is 'to die out and disappear'; but in the same book, outlining his programme for a future socialist utopia, he recommends the scientific killing of incurables, alcoholics and persons with transmissible diseases, all of whom will have to be 'removed from being'. This is a view highly compatible with *Das Kapital* and still more compatible with the totality of Marx's views recently unearthed by modern scholarship. But the problem of Wells's sources remains obscure. Wells did not regard himself as a

Marxist, though he was later to support with enthusiasm Lenin's seizure of power in October 1917. He drew on a wide variety of scientific–progressive views absorbed over a period of years into a highly individual philosophy. On the other hand, his version of racialism is strikingly like Marx's and Engels's in its contempt for the left-overs of history. Even as late as *The Science of Life* (1929–30), where he rejected talk about racial purity as nonsense, he dismissed 'certain very isolated peoples' in Africa, Australia and Brazil as 'divergent or retrograde forms of human life' – backward, conservative and fated to disappear one way or another.[22] But the prospect for planned genetic progress, by then, had waned, and Wells's *Work, Wealth and Happiness of Mankind* (1931) offers no easy hope. Scientists do not know enough, he had come to believe – or at least not yet.

In the following year (1932) J. B. S. Haldane enforced a similarly sceptical view in *The Inequality of Man,* a collection of previously published articles. These programmes for a scientific state, he believed, were still far in the future:

> The only clear task of eugenics is to prevent the inevitably inefficient one per cent of the population from being born, and to encourage the breeding of persons of exceptional ability where that ability is known to be hereditary. We cannot as yet go much further than this. . . .[23]

Months later, the National Socialists took power in Germany, and went much further indeed. But intellectual socialists in the West had already, by then, lost most of their racial certainties; and by a supreme irony of history they were forced to watch, powerlessly and from the sidelines, a drama for which they had written much of the script, performed by men they despised working in a cause they could not fathom.

★

The story of socialist racialism, then, among intellectuals born in the reign of Victoria, ended in scientific doubt and political embarrassment; and that embarrassment helps to explain how thorough an attempt was later to be made to brand racialism as a Fascist perversion.

On an historical view, however, all that is much too simple. Only some Fascist states have been racialist, after all; and not all socialist states, then or now, have escaped racialism. The obsessions of Victorian socialists survived in Stalin's policies towards minorities, and among those of his successors. And even, from time to time, and as the profoundest imaginable embarrassment, they appear in the protestations of some Marxist sects in the present age. In December 1972, for example, Ulrike Meinhof of the West German 'Red Army Fraction' came before a judicial hearing and spoke up publicly in the old cause of revolutionary extermination. 'How was Auschwitz possible, what was anti-semitism?', she asked from the dock:

> People should have explained all that, instead of accepting Auschwitz collectively as an expression of evil. The worst of it is that we were all agreed about it, Communists included.

But now she had recognised that 'anti-semitism was essentially anti-capitalist: it absorbed the hatred of men for their dependence on money as a means of exchange, and their longing for communism'. And she went on in passionate self-defence:

> Auschwitz meant that six million Jews were killed, and thrown on to the waste-heap of Europe, for what they were: money-Jews [*Geldjuden*]. Finance-capital and banks, the hard core of the system of imperialism and capitalism, had turned the hatred of men against money and exploitation, and against the Jews. The failure of the Left, of the Communists, had lain in not making these connections plain.

And so Marxism and racialism were proposed once more as philosophical comrades, the link again made plain:

> Germans are anti-semitic, and that is why they nowadays support the Red Army Fraction. They have not yet recognised all this, but only because they have not yet been absolved of fascism and the murder of the Jews. And they have not yet been told that anti-semitism is really a hatred of capitalism.[24]

They had been told it in the nineteenth century, however; they had been told it by Marx and Engels. And all Europe had been told it, by British socialists as well as by German, before 1914. If Europe has since contrived to forget it, it may yet contrive to remember. The reminder is just to the dead, and salutary to the living.

9 | *The Social Criticism of Matthew Arnold*

The years since 1950 have been marked by a surprising revival in the rhetoric of Victorian intellectual protest: surprising in the sense that the Forties, with that horror of totalitarianism characteristic of Hitler's age and Stalin's, had done little to foreshadow a renewed critique of liberal values in the old Victorian vein. The name of Matthew Arnold (1822–88) was suddenly potent again, in Britain and beyond. In 1951 a literary quarterly called *Essays in Criticism* was founded by F. W. Bateson in Oxford under a highly Arnoldian title, and the first issues took care to make its discipleship explicit. In 1953 John Holloway's *Victorian Sage* drew the attention of learned opinion to certain social critics of the age, mainly on rhetorical grounds, notably to Carlyle, Newman, Disraeli and Arnold; and in 1958 Raymond Williams's *Culture and Society 1780–1950* added more sages to the canon, including Cobbett, John Stuart Mill, Elizabeth Gaskell, Ruskin and Morris, along with the Fabians and some twentieth-century successors. This sudden outburst of literary enthusiasm had little enough to build on but the works of the Victorians themselves: an exception was Lionel Trilling's admiring study of Arnold (1939), which had uncritically accepted the greater part of his strictures on the Victorian world as just and accurate; and a few months earlier F. R. Leavis, in an article in *Scrutiny* entitled 'Arnold as Critic' (December 1938), had lauded his criticism as 'compellingly alive'. Such were the opening fanfares of a noisy chorus that was to deafen the Fifties and the Sixties.

The recent cult of the Victorian sage, and notably of Arnold, had one considerable consequence. It made a received literary doctrine of the view that Victorian England was an age of evil or, at the best, of profoundly mistaken social and cultural policies against which a few brave intellectuals heroically stood out. The arguments of Arnold and others, in this view, were not always invulnerable in detail. None the less, it was understood, the sages had been supremely in the right to choose the state of *culture* as their ground of debate; and if they had not spoken out, it is now widely assumed, the Victorian age would have abandoned itself to mere complacency and been left to wallow in the bland ethos of Dickens's Mr Podsnap. By now, in all probability, most students of literature take something like this for granted, and in literary circles in the Western world it would be thought highly paradoxical to argue that Victorian parliaments often understood social problems better, and combated them more effectively, than did Carlyle or Arnold or Ruskin. Even across the centuries, it seems, there is still a caste loyalty among men of letters, and it is never easy for literary critics to admit that they understand politics less well than the politicians. That would be a deflating admission, though it would be diverting to consider how critics would react to a politician who claimed to understand literature better than themselves. It is largely because of what Arnold and other Victorian sages wrote that the literary critic of today can argue in these terms without even noticing how confident his assumptions are. This is what Arnold, among others, did for English criticism. He gave it the confidence to see literature as the 'central' activity of the human mind, and to see the critic of literature as the lofty arbiter of all civilisation. The Arnoldian critic is a philosopher-king, in his own pretension, and not of literature alone. He aspires to intellectual and even moral authority over governments: not just as a citizen (which no democratic spirit would wish to deny him) but as an expert, and his claim to the expert's status is somehow thought to be based on his knowledge of literature and a burning conviction that such knowledge is a talisman to the whole world of human commitment.

Until recently this view, for all its boldness, has met with astonishingly little resistance. Historians of the nineteenth century can hardly have taken it seriously, but then they did not usually take literary critics seriously either; and they must often have thought the business of refuting all this to be beneath their notice. The real danger of Arnoldianism was not fully recognised until it was in almost full possession of the literary field and of much of our cultural life as well. That danger consists in the claim that literature tells the whole story, and tells it more or less accurately: that the Victorians are better revealed in Carlyle's *Past and Present*, for instance, or in

Arnold's social criticism, than in *Hansard* or the blue books. It is only recently that this astounding claim has been exposed to scrutiny. I wish now to expose it to still more searching scrutiny, and to consider Arnold's social criticism in terms of its historical accuracy. Did Arnold tell the truth? And did he even try to tell it?

★

Recent debate has done one useful service. It has recalled how neatly antithetical, at times, the Victorian intellectual situation was. The literary mind likes to see things in terms of black and white, and it is not always wrong to do so. Intellectual protest in the Victorian age was enormously various, but at least it was essentially directed against a single enemy: what Richard Oastler spiritedly called 'the same spirit which insults royalty, deludes and defames the aristocracy, degrades the clergy, robs and oppresses the working classes and insults women'. Raymond Williams, quoting this in his *Culture and Society*, restates it all in his own milder language: industrial capitalism, and . . . the limitations of triumphant middle-class liberalism'; and he goes on:

> One kind of conservative thinker, and one kind of socialist thinker, seemed thus to use the same terms, not only for criticizing a *laissez-faire* society, but also for expressing the idea of a superior society. This situation has persisted, in that 'organic' is now a central term both in this kind of conservative thinking and in Marxist thinking. The common enemy (or, if it is preferred, the common defender of the true faith) is Liberalism.[1]

That offers the choice of liberalism or conservative socialism, which is starker than anything Arnold openly offered. But it continues and completes the Arnoldian argument about the choices open to modern industrial states, and it is useful as a reminder of the kinship between conservative and Marxist thought. Socialism is almost wholly an invention of the Victorian mind, and its revolutionary claims should not allow one to forget that it was, like Toryism, a protest against a world being pushed by industrialism and political democracy too fast and too far. Ruskin and Morris, as surely as Disraeli and Carlyle, idealise the Middle Ages and the vanishing paradise of rural England. The Whig mind, like Macaulay's, was dedicated to movement and change in a direction already taken; the social critic, by contrast, saw utopia by a backward glance, nostalgically, and through a mist of fanciful history. For Arnold that utopia was not medieval but hellenic, and his gaze was fixed on Periclean Athens. But, like the rest of the sages, he hated the England that he saw and knew.[2]

All this is offered as a warning. It means that to limit knowledge of Victorian England to the works of the sages would be to listen to the voice of the prosecutor alone. Professor Williams, for example, believes that Victorian society was based on *laissez-faire*; and he believes this largely, no doubt, because it is widely believed; and more particularly because Carlyle in his essay on 'Chartism' (1839) has said so: 'That self-cancelling Donothingism and Laissez-faire should have got so ingrained into our practice is the source of all these miseries. . . .' And yet Lord Robbins's study, *The Theory of Economic Policy in English Classical Political Economy*, which appeared in 1952 – a book still too little known – has demonstrated with finality that Liberal economists have never in any age believed in *laissez-faire*; and later historians have shown that Victorian governments did not practise it or claim to practise it.

Laissez-faire is the doctrine that the function of the state is limited to that of the 'night-watchman', to the prevention of violence or theft and the assurance of certain basic human rights, and that in economic affairs the best that government can do is to stay out. It can be asserted with fair confidence that no British government, and indeed no British political party, has ever accepted that doctrine, or claimed to accept it, or behaved as if it accepted it. It is clearly foreign to the Benthamites, who prescribed numerous and elaborate functions for the state designed to further the greatest happiness of the greatest number. Adam Smith, the ancestor-figure of Liberal economic theory, knew the doctrine from French sources, and rejected it. In *The Wealth of Nations* (1776) he held that the state ('the sovereign', as he calls it) has three functions: first, defence; second, 'the duty of protecting, as far as possible, every member of the society from the injustice or oppression of every other member of it'; and third, 'the duty of erecting and maintaining certain publick works and certain publick institutions which it can never be for the interest of any individual, or small number of individuals, to erect and maintain; because the profit could never repay the expence', adding 'though it may frequently do much more than repay it to a great society'.[3] This third provision is of course in flat defiance of the principle of *laissez-faire*. And the mass of Victorian economic legislation after the first effective Factory Act of 1833 – the Poor Law reform of 1834, the public health measures of the 1840s and after, the creation of the penny post by Parliament in 1838, the creation of public libraries in the 1850s, the compulsory Vaccination Act against smallpox (1853), and the mass of social legislation set on foot by Gladstone after 1868, including universal education – all demonstrate that Carlyle's remark of 1839 is in the highest degree misleading. It is supremely ironical that the first age in our history successfully to limit by legislation the abuse of child labour should today be widely regarded as especially guilty of the exploitation of children. Students of literature are peculiarly vulnerable in situations like these. It is natural that they should respect literary evidence beyond all other kinds, and natural that they should know more about what Carlyle and Arnold wrote than about what Lord John Russell and Edwin Chadwick did. The plain fact is that we must stop assuming that the Victorian sages told the truth about their own society. In Arnold's case it is even probable that he knowingly and deliberately misrepresented the facts.

★

Arnold's use of contemporary evidence is now becoming available, much of it for the first time, through the researches of R. H. Super and the other editors of the *Complete Prose Works of Matthew Arnold*, which began to appear in 1960. The commentary to this edition offers a starting-point to these investigations, and no more than that; certainly the conclusions offered here concerning Arnold's intellectual integrity are in no way attributable to the Michigan editors. The range of investigation is vast, and the examples chosen here from the body of Arnold's prose have been selected mainly with a view to their notoriety. They are crucial in themselves, in the progress of Arnold's argument; but, equally important, they are crucial to the literary mythology of our own age, in the sense that they are repeatedly quoted not merely as examples of what Arnold thought of the Victorians, but as evidence of the nature of the age itself.

In the course of 'The Function of Criticism at the Present Time' (1865), an essay written as a provocative opening to the first series of

Essays in Criticism, Arnold holds up for contempt a Benthamite Member of Parliament, J. A. Roebuck, whom he reports as having used these words in a speech to his constituents in Sheffield:

> I look around me and ask, what is the state of England? Is not property safe? Is not every man able to say what he likes? Can you not walk from one end of England to the other in perfect security? I ask you whether, the world over or in past history, there is anything like it? Nothing. I pray that our unrivalled happiness may last.

Arnold's retort is forever famous: it is to

> confront with our dithyramb this paragraph on which I stumbled in a newspaper soon after reading Mr Roebuck: – 'A shocking child murder has just been committed at Nottingham. A girl named Wragg left the workhouse there on Saturday morning with her young illegitimate child. The child was afterwards found dead on Mapperly Hills, having been strangled. Wragg is in custody.'

And Arnold continues, in a vein of playfulness which even his best admirers have at times found difficult to justify, lamenting the lack of euphony in English surnames – 'by the Ilissus there was no Wragg, poor thing', and the lack of courtesy in police reports – 'the sex lost in the confusion of our unrivalled happiness'. But the passage is still a triumph of Arnoldian irony, taken as a whole; surely, one is meant to feel, the essential Podsnappery of Victorian culture was never so tellingly exposed as here.

Nobody in a hundred years has troubled to spring to the defence of Roebuck's Sheffield speech, though Asa Briggs in *Victorian People* (1954) has admiringly described his political activity during the Crimean War. He was a man of some literary gifts. Mill in his *Autobiography* (1873) was to reproach him for having mistakenly preferred Byron to Wordsworth in youth; though Roebuck's own fragmentary memoir, published posthumously in his *Life and Letters* (1897), offers a more convincing and more personal account of their early quarrel. Arnold's attack is so well executed that it may be impossible to reclaim Roebuck's reputation now, but certainly *The Times* report, on which Arnold's derision is presumed to have been based, leaves a decidedly different impression from 'The Function of

Criticism'. Arnold claims to have stumbled on the Wragg report 'soon after reading Mr Roebuck's', though the report of Roebuck's speech appears in *The Times* on 19 August 1864, and that of Elizabeth Wragg's trial on 15 March 1865, a matter of seven months later. The murder took place on 10 September 1864, some weeks after Roebuck made his speech, and one may wonder why Roebuck should be accused of having failed to mention an event which did not occur until weeks after he had spoken.

No doubt Arnold offers the story of infanticide as representative. But Roebuck's speech is certainly not Podsnappish or complacent. On the contrary, it is an ironic defence of a government which the Member in general supports, in spite of a certain lack of heroism he is far from denying. It records general assent with particular qualifications. The Prime Minister, Lord Palmerston, that 'very wise old gentleman' (a remark greeted, according to *The Times*, with 'cheers and laughter') has kept England out of the American Civil War and out of its apparent duty of defending Denmark against Prussia, and has been called the leader of a 'do-nothing' government in consequence. Roebuck makes it clear that, at the time of these events, he thought the government over-cautious on both counts; not a complacent argument, and one which excited the open amusement of his audience. But on reflection, Roebuck argues, Palmerston's caution was justified, though only just, by the peace and well-being of the nation at home. Foreign adventures, however attractive to a sense of justice, are not compatible with the existing level of prosperity, a prosperity in itself highly precarious; and the audience is urged to understand that the nation canot undertake everything at once. And the speech concludes not, as Arnold would have it,

> I pray that our unrivalled happiness may last,

but

> I pray that our unrivalled happiness may escape the terrible ending that the superstitious fear and tremble for. . . . You ought to be very careful how you decide that your representative ought to act. You are so happy, you are so distinguished from the rest of the world, that every step a wise man takes is taken with trembling and in terror lest he should, in any way whatever, render insecure that great happiness you enjoy, which the world sees and which the world envies.

Admittedly there is meat for Arnold here, and admittedly the speech is hardly a masterpiece of political eloquence. But considering that it is a speech made to his constituents by an M.P. who sits on the government side, Arnold is acting deviously in omitting the pleasant ironies against the Prime Minister which it contains; and he is clearly unjustified in changing the ending to suit his case better. Certainly it does not begin to justify the cheerful travesty that then follows in Arnold's essay:

> 'All Philistines together. . . . Let us have a social movement . . . let us call it *the liberal party,* and let us all stick together, and back each other up. Let us have no nonsense about independent criticism, and intellectual delicacy, and the few and the many; don't let us trouble ourselves about foreign thought; we shall invent the whole thing for ourselves as we go along. . . .'

This does not even possess the truth demanded of caricature. To suggest that Victorian Liberal thought was not exposed to foreign influence is plainly a nonsense. How could a party hostile to ideas have attracted into its active ranks such men as Mill, or Gladstone, or Acton; or John Bright, whose speeches, among the most successful examples of popular oratory in their day, are laced with quotations from Dante, Chaucer, Spenser, Shakespeare, Milton, Gray and Byron? And how does Arnold reconcile his view of the Victorian Liberals as inventing the whole thing as they went along with his own charge, so formidably made a few years later in *Culture and Anarchy* (1869), that the characteristic fault of the 'Philistines' was to be rigidly ideological, 'mechanical' and 'hebraistic' in their devotion to free trade and other 'stock notions'; or that they should rather 'turn a free and fresh stream of thought upon the whole matter in question'? Arnold's case is at variance not only with the evidence, but in this instance even with itself.

The case of *Culture and Anarchy* is beyond all others remarkable, since it is a work which has survived to be read – as no comparable work of Carlyle's or Mill's has so clearly survived – for the very purpose for which it was written: the study of English culture in its relation to society. It is the more important that the modern reader should attend carefully to Arnold's use of evidence. One dubious instance has long since been exposed by Dover Wilson in his admiring edition of 1932. In the preface Arnold had claimed to quote a passage from a speech by John Bright at Birmingham early in 1868, opposing government assistance to higher education on the grounds that the claims of universal primary education came first, and instancing the inventive faculty of the American people; and he simultaneously called for private philanthropy on behalf of technical education. This call was quickly answered by a private benefactor in the foundation of Mason University College (which eventually, in 1900, became the University of Birmingham). It is in no way offered as a speech about what Arnold calls 'the things of the mind', matters which Bright on other evidence held in high reverence. Arnold can be acquitted of the charge of deliberately misquoting Bright in the passage 'I believe the people of the United States have offered to the world more valuable information during the last forty years than all Europe put together', since it has been shown that the substitution of 'information' for 'inventions' was an error committed by *The Times* itself (6 February 1868). But he must have been aware that he was misrepresenting Bright in a general sense, since the report of the speech shows that its subject is limited to the immediate question of technical education, and that the Americans are being praised for their inventive faculty, not their 'culture and totality'. Arnold's use of the passage is unscrupulous in a high degree. 'I cannot do what I want', he once wrote to his mother, 'without, now and then, a little explosion which fidgets people.' The preface demonstrates how little he cared for the ordinary decencies of debate.

A larger and still more striking case may be more conclusive. In the sixth chapter of *Culture and Anarchy*, 'Our Liberal Practitioners', Arnold attacks various 'Nostrums' of current political Liberalism, including attitudes to free trade, the Irish Establishment, Bright's Intestacy Bill, the right to marry a deceased wife's sister. Arnold's argument here is necessarily oblique, since his concern is to show not that such proposals are mistaken, but rather that they are beside the point, 'Hebraising' rather than 'Hellenising'. It is a lordly argument, and Arnold nowhere explains how he would reform British society without passing bills framed in legal jargon and on subjects confined enough to be styled by parliamentary draftsmen. A full-blooded revolutionary, of course, would have his own drastic answer to all this; but Arnold was always very far from being that; and a House of Commons dedicated to hellenism is hard to imagine at work.

At one point in his argument he turns to attack *The Times* and its 'appointed doctors of free-trade', offering the following as a quotation from a *Times* report: 'Art is long, and life is short; for the most part we settle things first and understand them afterwards. Let us have as few theories as possible; what is wanted is not the light of speculation. . . .' This is from *The Times* of 7 July 1868, from a report on a conference on 'Laws of Labour' at which Gladstone, Sir James Shuttleworth, Ludlow and Ruskin had recently spoken. The report quotes Gladstone on the need for 'bringing about an harmonious union of interests' between employers and employed, and then complains: 'Men must be on the wrong track when, in approaching a purely practical matter, they find themselves suddenly involved in these labyrinths of speculation', and it goes on to insist that in economics theory follows practice, and that it must be fully based on a close observation of practice. There is no attack on theory as such in *The Times* report, but only on ignorant theorising; and its clear implication is that *The Times* does not consider that Gladstone, Ruskin and others have much practical experience of industry. Arnold represents the report as hostile to all speculation about the nature and purpose of society and complacent about the sufficiency of orthodox Liberal views.

Several pages later in the same chapter, Arnold returns to the attack on *The Times* with one of the most famous of all quotations, on the current crisis in the East End caused by economic depression and the early winter of 1867, ending: 'There is no one to blame for this; it is the result of Nature's simplest laws!' The passage is a gift to all who cherish the stony-faced image of Victorian Liberalism, and it is still quoted as a final indictment of the prevailing style of Victorian government; but even the Michigan editors are unable to find any trace of this passage in *The Times* itself. Either Arnold, who claims to have 'transcribed' it from that newspaper in order to 'fortify myself against the depressing sights which . . . assail us' when visiting the East End, has invented the passage; or else he has copied it from some so far undiscovered source and confused its origin. The latter proceeding might well be an honest one; but what is not is his suggestion that the passage, whether real or invented, represents the prevailing view of *The Times* and of similar opinion. In fact *The Times,* in a leader of 11 December 1867, had demanded that the existing level of private winter-help should be maintained, and that in addition the government should act in some more radical way to prevent the sufferings of the poor: 'Many causes combine to make their lot more than usually intolerable.' Even in good years, the leader-writer warned, there was always some destitution in winter, and the sufferings of the aged and the ill 'were urged upon the public attention, and always with success. In this work we have always borne an active part. The various institutions which have been founded for the relief of distress during the winter season have found in these columns their readiest means of publicity, as well as a constant and hearty advocacy.'

The Times then confronts the most difficult question of all. Given that private charity must continue at least at its present level, should it be encouraged to rise? The answer is a reluctant No, based upon the principle of the mobility of labour: 'the nature of the artisan's occupation ordains that he should be ready to strike his tent at the shortest notice, and go and dwell elsewhere as the market for this labour may vary.' And the leader ends by demanding state action to end destitution, presumably by assisting labour to become more mobile, rather than increased private charity:

> The poverty which reigns throughout this extensive region [of the East End] is plainly a matter which concerns, not parish clergymen and volunteer philanthropists, but the state. Parliament showed by the Act of last session [a reform of the Poor Law] that it was willing to deal thoroughly with questions relating to the London poor. Why should not the chronic destitution of Poplar or Bethnal-Green be treated with vigour?

Nothing about 'Nature's simplest laws' here, nothing open to the charge of complacency, and nothing that smacks of Do-nothingism.

★

Why is Arnold such an inaccurate critic of Victorian government and civilisation? It can hardly be a matter of ignorance. His reading was genuinely wide, even if it lacked the assiduity and care, the sheer scholarly readiness to be bored, of Sainte-Beuve, his acknowledged master in criticism; and his long career as an inspector of schools, which lasted for thirty-five years (1851–86), must have given him exceptional opportunities for social observation. And yet, when one considers the level of argument upon which Arnold conducted his polemics, it seems very remote from any concern with accuracy or fair-mindedness. The love of truth was something he appears to have outlived early. Remark the following, from the 1865 preface to *Essays in Criticism*:

> My vivacity is but the last sparkle of flame before we are all in the dark, the last glimpse of colour before we all go into drab – the drab of the earnest, prosaic, practical, austerely literal future. Yes, the world will soon be the Philistines' !

and consider at random what the previous five years of English literary civilisation had produced: *Great Expectations, Mill on the Floss, Gryll Grange, The Four Georges, The History of Civilization, Silas Marner, Evan Harrington, Representative Government, The Cloister and the Hearth, Early Italian Poets, Our Mutual Friend, Apologia pro vita sua, Enoch Arden, Sesame and Lilies, Atalanta in Calydon.* Not bad for Philistines, one is inclined to murmur.

But if Arnold was not ignorant of all this, or of much of it, another defence might be indulgently made for him: that his essays are radically diatribes, that they claim to describe, not Victorian culture as a whole, but only what is wrong with it. It would be right to give free rein to this hypothesis, but even those passages examined here include evidence to suggest that it is excessively charitable. When, after all, does Arnold ever hint at such a distinction? When does he except from his indictments any of the numerous and visible achievements of his age, or suggest, however faintly, that his generation had its victories as well as its tasks still unfulfilled? His language is commonly comprehensive: 'before we are all in the dark . . . before we all go into drab'. Perhaps this habitual exaggeration is the reason why his social criticism made so little impression on its own age. That age was very far from political complacency, as its record of reform can show, and it is odd to reflect that *Culture and Anarchy* appeared as a book during the first year of Gladstone's first ministry. Judicious contemporaries may well have thought it all too absurd to matter much. Henry Sidgwick, in a delicately derisive article in *Macmillan's Magazine* (August 1867) ironically entitled 'The Prophet of Culture', repeats a *Daily Telegraph* jibe against Arnold as the 'elegant Jeremiah', a phrase he calls 'tolerably felicitous for a Philistine', and runs on happily:

> Nor can I quite determine which Hebrew prophet Mr. Arnold does most resemble. But it is certainly hard to compare him to

Jeremiah, for Jeremiah is our type of the lugubrious; whereas there is nothing more striking than the imperturbable cheerfulness with which Mr. Arnold seems to sustain himself on the fragment of culture that is left him, amid the deluge of Philistinism that he sees submerging our age and country.

The Victorians probably had the measure of Arnold's rhetoric. 'Anarchy' did not perturb them because it so obviously did not perturb him; and they could well assert, without complacency, that through their own efforts social and cultural progress was in real measure a fact as well as an unending aspiration.

The critical reaction to *Culture and Anarchy,* chapters of which first appeared as articles in the *Cornhill* in July 1867 and after, was ambiguous in much the same way: admiration for Arnold's literary verve was often mixed with scepticism, even contempt, for his lofty conduct of an argument. 'Clever little barkings at the heels of the men who advance' was a phrase the *Daily Telegraph* had already employed about him (2 July 1867); and some outspoken journals used terms as dismissive as 'fribble' and 'the dandy Carlyle'.[4] An unsigned review by C. S. M. Phillipps in the *Edinburgh Review* (April 1869) quotes with disapproval the phrase 'elegant trifler', already used of Arnold, and pronounces him by contrast 'a consummate master of literary criticism'. But the reviewer adds: 'His critical works are a most provoking study. They are full of clever and original remarks; but the manner in which they overlook the plainest inferences and distinctions is so extraordinary as to make us suspect that two such different voices cannot really proceed from the same mouth.' That is a painstaking, literal view of the book. For a more searching scepticism, R. H. Hutton's reviews in the *Spectator* of 1867–8, which are among the most serious reactions to Arnold's doctrine of culture in his own day, are highly revealing evidence. The 'study of perfection' that Arnold calls for, Hutton gravely argues, could lead only to 'moral affectation' and 'aesthetic melodrama': 'We deny that the aesthetic culture which Mr. Arnold holds up before us as one of the highest conscious ends of existence can be attained by conscious pursuit at all' (6 July 1867). In a later article Hutton compares him with Carlyle, and in terms that leave little credit to Arnold's practical sense: 'If Mr. Carlyle makes an idol of action apart from knowledge, Mr. Arnold makes an idol of knowledge apart from action; and both seem to us to miss the vital relation between the two.' Such scepticism summarises a good deal of the contemporary view of Arnold. He was admired, in his own age, less as a mind than as an accomplished mannerist in prose.

Arnold's own reaction to this scepticism was complex, and in later life he adopted a mask of indifference, even of obstinacy, towards the views of others. Thomas Hardy, who met him in 1880, reported that he 'had a manner of having made up his mind upon everything years ago, so that it was a pleasing futility for his interlocutor to begin thinking new ideas, different from his own, at that time of day'. Though his urbanity was unfailing, his lack of promotion evidently rankled, and he assured Hardy 'deprecatingly' that he was nothing but 'a hard-worked school-inspector'.[5]

It is certain that he was not an inspector for so long by willing choice. 'Though I am a schoolmaster's son', he told his audience at his farewell dinner in 1886, 'I confess that school teaching or school inspecting is not the line of life I should actually have chosen. I adopted it in order to marry the lady who is here to-night.'[6] For years he had tried to escape that treadmill, and without success, as a series of letters requesting support in his applications for less arduous duties show. (See Appendix at the end of this chapter.) He believed that Gladstone had blocked his promotion,[7] and he seems to have been right; and Gladstone's reason for disliking him was evidently his unpopularity in Nonconformist circles. Hebraism, in fact, or the Nonconformist spirit, had deprived Arnold of promotion; and *Culture and Anarchy* and the social criticism that followed represent the punishment he tried to inflict, out of revenge, on the ruling party of state. He had inspected Nonconformist schools since 1851, and yet the very interest that ran those schools had blocked his way. In April 1867 he had sought the librarianship of the House of Commons; in December 1869, shortly after *Culture and Anarchy* had been collected as a book, he had failed to win a secretaryship in the Education Department; and in 1882–3 he was to be successively disappointed in his applications for seats on the Endowed Schools Commission and on the Charity Commission.[8] His department took a certain pride in his name, which added a literary lustre to their proceedings. But it seems clear that practical educational opinion did not trust his judgement. A year before Arnold's death, an experienced educationist was to accuse him publicly of having talked 'twaddle' about education and culture. 'What a pretty position of affairs', wrote James Runciman in *Schools and Scholars* (1887):

Mr. Matthew Arnold had been preaching and finicking in his exquisitely condescending way for years, but amid all his mincing talk about sweetness and light he never thought of bestowing a little sweetness and light on the young teachers whose interests he was paid to further. He is a good and charming man, but he certainly neglected his duty. A vigorous word from him to the [Education] Department would have brought about a complete change; as it is, all he ever did was to hold up one poor student to the mockery of the whole reading world simply because the unhappy lad made a ludicrous paraphrase of Shakespeare. Mr. Arnold apparently did not see that, while making game of the student in his kittenish way, he was condemning Her Majesty's senior inspector – that is, condemning himself.[9]

The charge is in substance the same as Hutton's. It is intellectual dandyism, or the frivolity that takes no care to match pretension with action.

Often something of a joke in his lifetime, if an affectionate one, Arnold was fated after death to become an irrelevance. Though he continued to enjoy the admiration of a few, including A. E. Housman,[10] his modern reputation is largely a creation of the years since the Second World War. Rupert Brooke, in a paper read to the Cambridge Fabians in 1910, *Democracy and the Arts* (published in 1946), saw him as the epitome of solemn Victorian admonition: '. . . an elderly man, explaining to a group of young people that the stuff of Art is being ruled out of life, black-whiskered and perplexed and in earnest – slightly resembling Matthew Arnold, a recurrent figure of most excellent comic value'.[11] Ezra Pound, at much the same time, thought him cold-blooded as a critic, and complained of 'his mind's frigidity': poetry, he remarked in passing in *The Spirit of Romance* (1910), 'is about as much a "criticism of life" as red-hot iron is a criticism of fire'.[12]

To the age of his successors the name of Arnold rang cold and dead. But the cultural anxieties of the 1950s and after, by a strange turn, have revived the glory of his name, the inaccuracies of his strictures on Victorian life being left to pass unnoticed, their motives unknown. Such is the power of literary revivalism. It would have astonished many of his contemporaries to learn that he could one day be accepted as a serious analyst of literature or education, and shocked them to discover that a craving for intellectual protest could convert their 'elegant trifler' into a figure of urgent consequence, the focus of an allegiance and the stuff of which faiths are made.

APPENDIX

Matthew Arnold to Chichester Fortescue,[1] *19 April 1867*
'You will have almost forgotten me, and you will say that I bring myself to your remembrance only to pester you. But I am applying for that delightful post, the Librarianship to the House of Commons;' and asks for a reference.

(Strachie MSS. 322, CP 3/56, Somerset County Record Office.)

Arnold to H. A. Bruce,[2] *13 December 1869*
On the promotion of R. R. W. Lingen from the Permanent Secretaryship to the Education Department to the Permanent Secretaryship to the Treasury: 'I don't know how far one of the Assistant Secretaries may be thought entitled to his place in the Education Department, or how far I might, in any case, be unacceptable to Lord de Grey[3] as Lingen's successor; – but you know the Office; I have served under you; you know my claims so far as I have any; and I am sure you will, if you can without impropriety do so, speak to Lord de Grey in my favour. I apply to no-one else besides you, because Forster,[4] from his connection with me, cannot well stir in the matter, and except you and Forster, I know of no-one whose representations, in such a case as this, would be likely to have any weight with Lord de Grey.'

(Bruce MSS. in the possession of Lord Aberdare.)

1. Chichester Fortescue, Chief Secretary for Ireland 1868–71, created 1st Lord Carlingford 1874: Lord President of the Council 1883–5, and therefore the senior minister responsible for education, and in sole charge of the patronage of the appointments to the Education Department and the Inspectorate.

2. Henry Austen Bruce, Vice-President of the Committee of Council on Education 1864–7, and therefore junior minister, and the minister in the Commons responsible for education: Home Secretary 1868–73; created 1st Lord Aberdare 1873; Lord President of the Council 1873–4.

3. Earl de Grey and Ripon, Lord President of the Council 1868–73; created 1st Marquess Ripon 1871.

4. W. E. Forster, Vice-President of the Committee of Council on Education 1868–74, and Arnold's brother-in-law.

W. E. Forster to Lord de Grey, 14 December 1869
Matthew Arnold has informed him of his candidature for the Permanent Secretaryship: Forster therefore thinks it best that he should not communicate with Lord de Grey on the subject of the appointment at all.
(Ripon MSS. British Library Add. MSS. 43, 536 ff.237–8.)

W. E. Forster to Lord de Grey, 16 October 1872
Proposes Arnold as an inspector of training colleges on the retirement of the Rev. B. M. Cowie.
(Ripon MSS. British Library Add. MSS. 43, 537 ff.51–2.)

Arnold to Lord Spencer,[5] *2 March 1882*
Mundella[6] is pushing Arnold's name forward, for the vacancy on the Endowed Schools Commission: does he have Lord Spencer's support?
(Spencer MSS. Althorp.)

Chichester Fortescue, Lord Carlingford, to Lord Spencer, 21 June 1882
He has spoken to Mr. Gladstone about the possibility of giving the vacant Charity Commissionership to Arnold: 'I should be very glad indeed to see so distinguished a literary man and educationist placed in so suitable a position.' But he has no great hopes of this.
(Spencer MSS. Althorp.)

J. R. Dasent[7] *to Lord Spencer, 21 June 1882*
Arnold is offering himself for the Chief Inspectorship left vacant by C. J. Robinson's death.
(Spencer MSS. Althorp.)

E. W. Hamilton[8] *to Lord Carlingford, 16 April 1883*
Mr. Gladstone has been forced to reject the name of Arnold as a Charity Commissioner: 'The appointment would, Mr. Gladstone

5. 5th Earl Spencer, Lord President of the Council 1880–3.
6. A. J. Mundella, Vice-President of the Committee of Council on Education 1880–5.
7. J. R. Dasent, Examiner in the Education Department and Private Secretary to Lord Spencer as Lord President.
8. E. W. Hamilton, Private Secretary to Gladstone 1880–5.

feels sure, give considerable offence among Nonconformists ... '
        (Strachie MSS. 324, CP1/211, Somerset County Record
Office.)

Arnold was appointed to none of these jobs; he was finally made a
Chief Inspector in 1884, two years before his retirement.

10 | *Acton's 'History of Liberty'*

The liberalism of mid- and late-Victorian Britain, which Arnold made a chief target of his sarcasm, is the clearest and brightest instance in modern times of a political movement whose roots are literary. Its leader, Gladstone, was himself an active man of letters. Its novelists, such as Dickens, Thackeray, Trollope and Meredith, engaged fitfully in political life; its poets, above all Robert and Elizabeth Barrett Browning, wrote lavishly in its praise. It was always an adversary too large for Arnold and the rest of the sages to damage much, or even hope to damage much; and in the years between Gladstone's first ministry in 1868 and the Armistice year of 1918 it was more often in office than out.

But its grand masterpiece of historical revelation, Acton's 'History of Liberty', which he conceived in the 1870s, obstinately remained unwritten. The gap is not total, since fragments survive. In this chapter, which is based on a study of his manuscript notes, I shall expound Acton's defence of Gladstonism as a universal theory of morals and of history.

★

In 1872, as a young man in Paris, Henry James wrote a tale called 'The Madonna of the Future'. It tells of an American painter in Florence who worked obsessively on his masterpiece as his model aged into her middle years, leaving only a blank canvas at his death. No brush stroke, in the end, could equal his notion of the perfection he had contemplated.

The story was to haunt Lord Acton when shortly after, as a man of forty, he began to collect materials for a panorama of Western civilisation conceived as a history of liberty. James's story came to look increasingly apt. In 1880 Mary Gladstone, the Prime Minister's daughter, drew his attention to it;[1] and soon Acton, accepting the parallel humorously or ruefully, came in his letters to call the unwritten book his Madonna of the Future. But the analogy, self-lacerating as it was, is in the end unfair. The artist's portrait in the story was never even begun. For twenty years, by contrast, Acton kept pen to paper, accumulating a hoard of reading and of original observation drawn from the literatures of six languages and the reflections to which his study had given rise in his mind. A great cosmopolitan historian was seeking to memorialise an idea of history in the service of Gladstonian politics. His contemporaries, with rare exceptions, were not to know of it; his successors, after his death in 1902, were to see it only as a glorious phantom. 'The greatest book that was never written', one Edwardian Liberal was soon to call it. The papers were deposited in the University Library at Cambridge, where he had served the last seven years of his life as professor of modern history, and have lain there unpublished ever since.

The causes of Acton's failure have often been debated. Acton was not without practical sense, to speak generally, though his career in the world of affairs had been brief and inconclusive. He had sat as a Liberal in the Commons for an Irish seat from 1859 till 1865, in which year he narrowly failed to be elected for Bridgnorth in Shropshire, where he lived; whereupon Gladstone, who admired his intellectual powers, had sent him to the Lords. His background was cosmopolitan almost beyond parallel, and he merits as no other historian before or since the title of a European. Born in Naples in 1834, where his grandfather had been Prime Minister, reared by a French-speaking German mother in Shropshire and schooled as a Catholic in France and England, he became Döllinger's pupil in Munich in 1850, and from 1859 combined the careers of a Member of Parliament and a Catholic journalist and editor. By the 1870s his acquaintance with the world of European politics and letters was already vast beyond belief. It is not even clear what his native language was, though English and German seem to have come to him most easily as a correspondent. As an organiser of the anti-papal faction of bishops at the Vatican Council of 1870, when his party failed to defeat the Infallibility Decree, he had worked tirelessly, if often unsuccessfully, in more than one campaign that called for subtlety and resource.

In 1875, a few years after his defeat in Rome, he began his

'History of Liberty'. He cannot have been altogether ignorant of the dangers that confront all extended acts of authorship. He may even have been aware to excess of the historian's temptation to amass materials endlessly without formal composition. Incompletion had been a bugbear of his youthful mind. At the age of sixteen he had precociously observed of his master Döllinger that he 'appears to have in some degree the imperfection of neglecting to complete what he has begun'.[2] Years later, in an article of 1890 devoted to his old teacher, he reviewed the same temptation from the wisdom of experience: 'His collections constantly prompted new and attractive schemes, but his way was strewn with promise unperformed, and abandoned from want of concentration. He would not write with imperfect materials, and to him the materials were always imperfect.'[3]

But accumulation, after all, was the basis of the historical method Döllinger had trained him in. For all his life as an historian, Acton knew no other and respected no other. 'I have no other gift', he wrote to Mary Gladstone in 1884, 'but that which you pleasantly describe – of sticking bits of paper into innumerable boxes. There is no help for it'.[4] A habit once formed and sanctioned by the example of his master was to last him till his death. But it was always much more than a habit. It was the only method countenanced by historians of an advanced temper in his own times. And though since criticised and altered, it has not been superseded. The two cardinal sins of scholarship in its technical aspects remain to this day an ignorance of what needs to be known and a needless insistence on what is already known. Acton's warnings are still salutary. The trouble with Buckle's *History of Civilisation,* he remarked tartly in 1858, soon after its first volume appeared, was that Buckle had 'taken great pains to say things that have been said much better before in books he has not read'.[5] A craving for documentation was not a superstition: it rested on intelligible motives, at once aspiring and cautious. He could not supplant it as a method. But in the end its demands were to defeat him.

At Acton's death the 'History of Liberty' lay unfinished: accumulated, even perhaps arranged, but substantially unwritten, an enormous monument to literary procrastination. There had always been something else to do. His last years at Cambridge had been devoted to the obsessively meticulous task, as he interpreted it, of planning the *Cambridge Modern History,* and he seems to have gone on accumulating his own notes to the end, or nearly so. The last dated entry in the surviving slips clearly devoted to the 'History of Liberty' refers to the year 1894, just before he took up his chair; so that he may have been amassing notes for a matter of twenty years.

And yet the enterprise was not useless even in Acton's lifetime. The body of his published and publishable writings, including the lectures and articles that appeared in highly finished prose soon after his death, is not really small for a man who engaged in public causes and died in his sixties. Though he left the greater part of his papers to be published or collected by colleagues after his death, his completed work is inconceivable without the support of his accumulated notes. He had used time unsparingly, but he had not wasted it. There is plenty to show, even apart from the articles of his early and middle years and the lectures he delivered at Cambridge in the last seven. Early in 1877, after little more than a year of work on the history, he delivered in Shropshire two lectures of the densest and most exacting erudition before the presumably undemanding audiences of the Bridgnorth Institution in the Agricultural Hall, in the very constituency that had omitted to elect him into Parliament a dozen years before. They were entitled 'The History of Freedom in Antiquity' and 'The History of Freedom in Christianity'; and together with the long review of Erskine May's *Democracy in Europe*, which he wrote for the *Quarterly Review* at the same time, they amount to a sizeable and considered treatise – an early realisation of an historical masterpiece which, in the event, was never to find any riper form than this. Nor did they lie unpublished at the time, though the manner of their publication was wayward in the extreme: the two Bridgnorth lectures appeared as threepenny pamphlets, and were reported verbatim at the same time in the weekly *Bridgnorth Journal* for March and June 1877; publication so casual as to make it practically certain that Acton saw them as no more than provisional and preparatory.

The occasion of the Bridgnorth lectures is worth consideration. They were written and delivered in an atmosphere of mounting Gladstonian fervour at the mid-point of Disraeli's second ministry of 1874–80. Two years later, the Midlothian by-election of 1879 was to return Gladstone to the Commons. The electoral mood of 1877 was less heady, but the lectures are clearly designed to excite political fervour and furnish an historical manifesto for a Liberal victory. Men of letters, even when former Members of Parliament, do not often behave in this way, and Acton's motives are worth some reflection.

Professional historians may be inclined to mock at the spectacle of a scholar of European eminence presenting his conclusions in the agricultural hall of a small county town. Acton himself did not think so. His declared object was to create and inform a body of opinion that would bring down a Conservative administration. The measure in which he succeeded is hard to judge and may well have been small, but his excitement over the election of 1880, which returned Gladstone to power, showed that he was not disappointed. According to the local newspaper report, his audience in 1877 was 'large and fashionable'; it interrupted him with frequent bursts of applause; and the chairman, at the end of his first lecture, thanked him for having treated the history of ancient liberty 'in so popular a manner'. All this requires some readjustment in our understanding. But the generation that made a best-selling novelist of George Eliot may not have found Acton academically remote as a public speaker, and it is easy now to underestimate the readiness of Victorian audiences to absorb speeches, sermons and lectures of massive length and subtle argumentation. The chairman's speech leaves no doubt that the lecture was a political occasion: 'Living under the freest constitution in the world, to anyone in this country the question of Freedom must be extremely interesting' (applause); and Acton, rising to reply to a vote of thanks, promised his audience that in his second lecture he would show 'how it came to pass, two hundred years ago, that the political development of the Western world seemed doomed to fail, and an invincible despotism was established in almost every country, in the systems of philosophy, and in the selfish aspiration of men'. All that refers to the regressive era of the Stuarts in England and of Louis XIV in France. But the English Revolution of 1689, and the defeat of France by its heirs early in the eighteenth century, were to call hope out of despair: 'And lastly it will be my happier task to tell how, in the midst of universal darkness, a light was kindled in a land encompassed by the inviolate sea which has shown ever since as a beacon to the nations.'[6]

Acton was to fulfil that promise, though delayed by illness, within three months. His purpose is unmistakable. This is the authentic voice of popular liberalism victoriously linked to patriotic fervour. The occasion was not merely or mainly academic. A scholar and journalist of European reputation, recently embarked on what promised to be his greatest work, had staked its first draft in the service of a political leader and the cause he led. The long friendship of Gladstone and Acton, that model of ardent sympathy between statesman and scholar, was in the event to find no more enduring monument than this.

★

How was it that Acton turned, and so decisively, from the Vatican organiser of 1869–70 into the advocate of a popular movement in one country; from youthful Whiggery into the most dedicated of ideological Liberals? The published lectures and reviews, together with the unpublished notes of the 'History of Liberty',[7] demonstrate how that double conversion occurred, and offer abounding detail for the study of Acton's mature convictions.* In 1850 he had arrived in Munich, a sixteen-year-old English schoolboy with a copy of Gibbon and a head full of the checks-and-balances theory of the British constitution. A quarter of a century later, when he took up his work on the 'History of Liberty', he had come to believe in the absolute morality of political ideas, that foundation-stone of Gladstonian Liberalism; a total ideologue only occasionally involved, by now, in the life of the Court or of Westminster, and a wandering scholar as much at home in Bavaria or the French Mediterranean as in England.

The shift from Whig to Liberal is justified at length in the notes. That is the grand theme of his life, as of the masterpiece he aspired to write. It had been propelled by more causes than one: a deep revulsion, as a Catholic apologist of the 1860s, from the anti-liberal policies of Pio Nono; a profound and agonising reflection over what the new papal policy signified in view of the long and chequered history of the popes; the vital personality of Gladstone in his emerging role as a popular orator in the decade that made him leader of his party, uniting moral purpose with scholarly passion in the new political art of demagogy; and a cast of mind that was in itself increasingly extreme and absolute. 'I have studied politics very elaborately', he wrote to John Henry Newman, as early as 1861, 'and more as a science than people generally consider it, and therefore I am afraid of writing like a doctrinaire, or of appearing to force a particular and very unpalatable system down people's throats.'[8]

*Unless otherwise indicated, ensuing phrases and passages or Acton's are quoted from the unpublished material specified in Note 7 to this chapter.

That fear was to diminish. As he grew older, as in his uncompromising Cambridge inaugural *The Study of History* (1895), he came to trust his convictions better, to feel their urgency and to accept the duty of proclaiming them; and soon he became bold. Quarrels with his old masters in France and Germany in the early 1880s, in the wake of the Infallibility Decree, were to embitter his temperament and make him ever more extreme. The notes on liberty, like the Bridgnorth lectures of 1877, are composed in support of a great party of state. But in many ways, as Acton rightly feared, they run far beyond the ordinary purposes of party and the humdrum context of British parliamentary life. The pen of the lonely and obsessive scholar knows little of compromise. If merged into a book, all this could only have proved an immortal manifesto recording the heyday of Victorian liberalism. But it would also have been something more and something other: a cry of pain from a mind agonised at the reluctance of men to face the consequences of their faith without flinching, and their lamentable eagerness to accept makeshift arguments that reconcile and mollify, but do not stand the test of truth.

★

Acton's theory of politics, like Gladstone's politics, is grounded on the objectivity of the moral law. There, in his own insistent view, lay the essential difference between the old Whig and the new Liberal. For all his virtues, the Whig had been a pragmatist: always 'short of theory', content with solving problems as they arose, and largely indifferent to the demands of higher principle. The men who had dominated public life for so much of the century that followed the revolution of 1689 had admired clarity more than profundity, and clarity in the end is only 'a French disease'. Their 'belief in mere logic' is something that lasted down into early Victorian times, to Cobden and Macaulay, and it was to render them ultimately superficial: 'They declared nothing they could not make clear to everybody. Revelled in commonplace. You must be understood by very plain men. A meaning that does not stare you in the face is no meaning at all.'

From Locke to Macaulay, from the Revolution of 1689 to the emerging democratic constitution of the 1860s, Acton saw a tradition of limited scope and superseded use. Its merits had been real enough, in its day. The Whig mind had rightly perceived that the English Civil War had been a mistake. The constitutional question which that war had tried and failed to solve could be 'set at rest, as long as land predominated'. By 1689, it was clear, king, lords and prelates were neither to be abolished altogether nor yet restored to the powers they held before 1642: 'Best that they should be preserved, but under such conditions as made them inoffensive'. The Whigs had made themselves, in their limited way, an aristocratic party of liberty; and they had defeated absolutist France and created the colonial constitutions of North America. No historical issue received more exhaustive treatment in Acton's notes than this. The 'History of Liberty', had it been written, would have been mainly concerned with England after its opening chapters, and mainly with the two centuries that stretch from the Civil War to the advent of Gladstone.

With the new Liberal, by contrast, begins 'the reign of ideas'. The Liberal is not a pragmatist, like the Whig, and he is not bound by respect for an existing order or the mere continuance of institutions. That is because he dares to give to moral reflection its true weight. 'A Liberal feels no reverence for the ancient order: it is a system of murder, organised, defined, proclaimed.' The new doctrine 'admits the dominion of conscience, less impeded by authority, reputation and time'. It has little commitment to compromise. The 'Whig draws the line somewhere; not so a Liberal. Nationality, democracy, property only sacred subsidiarily'. Acton's task in his later chapters was to take stock of what the Liberal claim to a morality of politics must mean, now and in the future, within the frontiers of the nation that had nurtured it and beyond them too. The history would not have stopped with the present, or limited itself to the ordinary bounds of historical narration. 'Study politics both as a national science and as a general science', Acton urged himself. The new doctrine, being irreverent, is enquiring and curious. 'One set of people will always ask what is the law: others, what ought to be the law.' To be bound by nationality, then, as a political thinker and historian, may restrict, may torify, the mind; but to be conversant with all political thinking, American, French, Swiss, German, English, must destroy Conservatism. Britain is the centre-point of the history, but not the limit; and what a Liberal exemplifies is true for all the world, in Acton's contention, and true for scholarship as for politics: 'Liberalism is not only a principle of government but a philosophy of history.'

The link between liberty and the moral law has so often been mis-understood, and is so naturally susceptible to misunderstanding, that it is proper for Acton's ideological insistence to lie powerfully here. It has always been easy to suppose that liberty means the absence of restraint, and that the absence of restraint means in its turn the right to do as you please. The greatest documents of the Victorian age, like the minds that composed them, were working earnestly towards an opposite conclusion: the speeches and treatises of Gladstone, the novels of George Eliot, and the treatises of John Stuart Mill, Acton and T. H. Green. Liberty, as Acton was fond of reiterating, is not the right to do as you please but the chance to do as you ought. No act, when constrained by another, can fully and freely represent a moral choice, and it is only when restraint is lifted that morality begins fully to operate. That is why, in the belief of many intelligent men, concessions made under duress are not bind-ing; and why honest men, under dire circumstance, may justifiably lie to save themselves and others. 'How they try to separate them', Acton exclaims indignantly: 'to found liberty on rights or enjoy-ments, not on duties. Insist on their identity. Liberty is that condition which makes it easy for conscience to govern.' It is not, in consequence, an easy choice for men of facile views, and it is a world away from mere permissiveness. Liberty makes a severe and stringent demand upon the individual conscience; among all the possible forms of social organisation, it stands supreme as the only one in which the moral duty can flourish. Doctrines like conser-vatism or socialism, by contrast, being based on acquiescence, deference, or obedience to the state or to combinations such as trade unions – all doctrines of central planning, in short – atrophy the moral sense and pervert the conditions in which virtue can thrive. The credulous may at times invoke authority, and on the best of motives, to plan their lives and censor their books. But in the end authority can only pervert, whether papal or secular.

This is the stage in Acton's argument where the powerful link between politics and religious sentiment was forged. Powerful and yet – as an observer might allow himself to comment – paradoxically inessential, since liberalism seems capable of coexisting actively and without strain with Acton's Romanism, Gladstone's High Churchmanship, the evangelical faith of countless British electors, and the high-minded infidelity of intellectuals like Mill or George Eliot. Acton called liberal morality the doctrine that 'lets God work', though God here might as reasonably stand for the moral convictions of the honest doubter and the enlightened infidel:

> . . . not restraining His action with fixed barriers. It is the liberty of Providence they demand. God's chief means of action on man is grace; and grace is individual. Expose the individual to that alone. Do not bury the conscience beneath the ruins of crumbled ages, and set the thrones on sepulchres – snatch the sceptre from the grasp of the dead.

So God might be called the supreme Liberal, in this view, his demands being always on the individual; and the moral sense in the end can only be a matter for the single conscience. This is the most inward and passionate of all the reflections that lie buried in Acton's unpublished papers. 'Men cannot be made good by the state, but they can easily be made bad', he wrote in another note. 'Morality depends on liberty.' But Acton could also perceive, as from afar, an element in his political creed that was ultimately destructive, if not of religion itself, at least of the church. Liberalism is an irreverent faith, and ultimately subversive. 'Liberalism looks to the future, and to what ought to be; makes ruins, if necessary; eventually irreligious', he wrote in one musing note. What lies on the other side of the liberty of moral choice could at moments look alarming.

Before liberalism, mankind had never dared to invest political thought with the full consequences of moral knowledge. Gladstone is a name often mentioned in Acton's letters, though seldom in his private notes, but he is the manifest hero of the projected history. It is he who saw morality as an aspect of knowledge and dared to apply that conviction, in the context of a popular movement, to the immediate and urgent tasks of British political life. For moral relativism, of a kind he believed he saw in Buckle's *History of Civilization,* Acton always had the profoundest contempt. It was by this evasion that popes, among others, had defended their worst atrocities, and by which Machiavelli, that arch-devil of political thought, had defended judicial murder and even murder itself. Morality is a kind of knowledge; and like other kinds, it progresses. There is 'no difference between moral and intellectual progress. Progress in ethical knowledge is part of intellectual progress'. As men learn more about morality, they organise and accumulate that knowledge better, much as historians and scientists do with the knowledge that is theirs. This is one of George Eliot's profoundest perceptions, and it is unsurprising that Acton admired *Middlemarch* so highly. The novel is above all a penetrating analysis of the motives that lead men to act: 'George Eliot seems to me capable not only of reading the divers hearts of men, but of creeping into their skin, watching the world through their eyes, feeling their latent background of conviction, discerning theory and habit, influences of thought and knowledge, of life and of descent. . .'.[9]

The relation between theory and habit is indeed what is in question here. Liberalism stands in the van of that progress, and dares to insist that to know the difference between right and wrong is indeed a kind of knowing, and no mere matter of private opinion; and it dares in its social and foreign policies to apply that knowledge to the course of events themselves. Those who imagine that confidence to be dogmatic have not sufficiently enquired into the nature of moral dogmatism. It is precisely the dogmatist who is least likely to allow that morality is a matter of knowledge, with all that this implies concerning the assembling of evidence and a readiness to attend to criticism. It is precisely the cognitive process – that of accumulating, organising and interpreting evidence – that is not dogmatic. To assert that something is known is to imply that it might, on later evidence, be shown to be false. That is how incontestably objective enquiries such as the natural sciences advance; and that is why the quest for moral knowledge is so tightly linked to the demand for civic liberty, with its right to assert, question and demolish.

> If truth is not absolute, then liberty is the condition of truth. Men got to believe that absolute truth is unattainable; only relative, only proximate. Bacon. That assures the reign of liberty: one motive for toleration.

★

Modern political thought in Britain, in Acton's unwavering view, was built on the imposing foundations of seventeenth- and eighteenth-century political thought. His history, had it been written, would have begun in ancient times and embraced the Middle Ages, and its scope would have been European and North American, with its emphasis on the failure of the Stuarts and the success of the Whig oligarchy after 1689 in guiding a nation peacefully towards the light of constitutional liberty. What Mac-aulay, a quarter of a century before, had performed for the dying cause of Whiggism in his *History of England* (1849–61), chronicling with sublime confidence a cause already at the point of decease, Acton would have performed for the Liberals who had inherited their role with Palmerston's death in 1865. At its greatest extent, Acton's history would have been an admiring critique of Locke, Burke and Macaulay, and a fanfare for the new political faith that had so recently swept them and their kind forever into a limbo of history.

The philosophical pioneer of Whiggism was Locke, and for Acton his memory was ambiguous with the splendour of a defunct tradi-tion. The triumphs of eighteenth-century England at home and abroad had been massively based on his thought. 'Chatham founded his politics on Locke', and the achievements of the oligarchy that followed 1689 were not to be belittled. But Locke's very success was ultimately stultifying: he had 'arrested political thought in England, by satisfying it, for two generations', and it was not until Hume and Burke that the British political mind, having digested the *Two Treatises of Government* (1690), could advance again. Locke had devis-ed a rationale for an aristocracy of real ability working inside an an-cient and ceremonial constitution: he 'believed in aristocracy, feared democracy'; and he had seen in an hereditary property-owning class a body of experienced governors, both local and national, that could be trained to serve a national purpose: 'Locke . . . connects liberty with wealth, and thinks power depends on the right of making laws for regulating and preserving property,' a presumption followed by some of the American colonies in their early constitutions. His was a concept of limited tolerance which excluded only atheists and Catholics, the state being 'an agreement for mutual protection, on the understanding that only the general welfare will be consulted', but largely indifferent to the principle of representation and always limited in its scope.

But Locke's notion of government had been one that 'deals only with material things, not with opinions'. It was tolerant as a matter of practice rather than of principle. Such was the cautiously devised compromise that served as a long transition between Stuart tyranny and modern democracy, and it was the best that any European nation could then achieve. Its exclusion of opinion from the business of state, broadly considered, had given a real freedom of opinion, not tenuous but precious freedom that the Whig oligarchy had conferred upon a nation bitter with memories of civil war and James II. In Britain its doctrine was a reality, and it was to become a potent influence on much of Europe; Locke 'kindled the light which the great literary intellect of Montesquieu spread over the continental world'. But Locke had none the less accepted the duty of the state to persecute any faith dangerous to itself, and he had tolerated slavery: both views that demonstrated how inadequate Whiggism must prove to the conscience of the nineteenth century. He remained a great if tarnished memory, the architect of modern political science in his separation of the political from the religious; and modern liberty took its rise from him.

The second great progenitor of liberalism was Burke. He had made the new ideology possible; it might almost be said that he made ideology possible. Others had defended and interpreted the historical past as men of leisure, a 'satisfied class' of thinkers. But 'not so with Burke – he really had a doctrine'. Acton's view of Burke must seem radical, perhaps even incredible, to a century that has commonly seen him as a proponent of the conservative idea. Acton believed that, as the years passed, Burke tended to become less and less Whig but not more and more conservative. His reputation, as he believed, had been distorted by an excessive emphasis on his *Reflections on the Revolution in France* (1790), that overrated work; even within the body of his last and most revolution-haunted writings, Acton preferred that more penetrating exercise in the analysis of free institutions, *An Appeal from the New to the Old Whigs* (1791). But Burke's mind could never admit what Acton called 'the American principle', or a right of self-government – only the right to good government; and it could not admit it because of Ireland.

> To admit the American principle was to revolutionize Ireland, and to bring about Reform. Burke could not revolutionize Ireland, and so resisted the American principle. And therefore he opposed reform. But why did he still oppose Reform after yielding to America? On account of Ireland.

So Ireland had already proved the graveyard of one hope, at least, for British liberty: an ironic reflection to any historian writing in the 1880s, with the spectacle of Gladstone's Home Rule policy before his eyes.

Acton did not live to see the electoral triumph of 1905–6, and his view of the future of democracy, like Gladstone's, was in any case unoptimistic. It is one of the wildest myths concerning Gladstonian liberalism to suppose it believed in its own inevitable triumph around the world, or even at home. Just the reverse is true. Both men knew that freedom might have only a short day, even in its Anglo-Saxon homelands. It was something to be won with difficulty, if at all, and held through sacrifice. Liberty they saw as the slow-maturing fruit of a long civilisation, and one not easily transplanted. 'Liberals admit that men are not always ripe for freedom.' One of Acton's favourite adages is from Schopenhauer, and he quotes it in a political context: 'Truth has only a short day, between paradox and the trivial'; and he saw freedom surviving 'in corners' of the world, if at all, in mountain regions, islands and colonies. 'It has to struggle with the reign of sin, with the dead and the living.' It is far indeed from a natural condition of man. One of his notes, headed 'Failure of Democracy', sadly lists Spain; Italy, where freedom was 'absorbed by monarchy'; France, where it had 'failed in 1851 with applause of Liberal men' through the accession of Napoleon III; and Switzerland which had proved itself 'untrue to it', while 'its appearance in Germany [is] stained with crime'. Acton was not one for easy hopes. 'In our time, only a precarious existence,' he concluded, viewing the threatening spectres of socialism and monarchy. If he had lived into the twentieth century and seen the emergence of monarchical socialism like Stalin's or Mao's, he might have felt himself doubly justified. The demand of Gladstonism is to act while there is time to act; to take no victory for granted, and to reform while it is yet day. Acton's ultimate justification for democracy is the most cautious that is conceivable, and it offers no ready prizes: 'It is easier to find people fit to govern themselves than people fit to govern others.' It is not that men govern themselves well. It is simply that they govern others worse.

★

Acton's failure to write his 'History of Liberty' has not always been charitably regarded, and some of the judgements of fellow-historians have a harsh, even derisive ring. In the first volume of *A Study of History* (1934), Arnold Toynbee saw the crisis as more than personal, and cast Acton as a victim of the industrialism that had cruelly dominated his century, a doomed factory-worker crushed by the mills of historical scholarship: 'one of the greatest minds among modern Western historians, in whose career the sterilizing influences of industrialism upon historical thought is tragically apparent' (p. 46). But industry is intolerant of process without end, and commonly completes and markets what it makes; and Acton himself, in any case, knew what it was to finish an article, a lecture and even, more rarely, a book. Toynbee's explanation is not convincing; the less so when one considers Acton's own ecstasy in contemplating the master-idea of his intellectural life. Nothing could sound less mechanical. 'Twenty years ago', wrote Bryce, recalling the 1880s,

> late at night, in his library at Cannes, he expounded to me his view of how such a history of Liberty might be written, and in what wise it might be made the central thread of all history. He spoke for six or seven minutes only; but he spoke like a man inspired, seeming as if, from some mountain summit high in air, he saw beneath him the far-winding path of human progress from the dim Cimmerian shores of prehistoric shadow into the fuller yet broken light of the modern time. . . . It was as if the whole landscape of history had been suddenly lit up by a burst of sunlight.[10]

A more recent historian has since taken a view diametrically opposed to Toynbee's, and one even harder to swallow: that Acton was at heart an amateur, or at best a mediocrity – 'an indifferent historian, often surprised by the discovery of intrigue or double-dealing behind an official façade into a somewhat amateurish re-action: astonishment at the commonplace, over-emphasis on the insignificant, heavily moral attitudes'.[11] But none of these constitutes a reason for failing to write a book, and not all of them are grave charges. A faculty for being surprised is not a defect, and Acton's case for seeing morality as an essential element in the fabric of the past is one he argues too cogently to be dismissed in a phrase. Acton's reply to all this is easily imagined. Any claim by the historian to cynicism, in the sense of existing above or beyond morality, is as much a moral claim as the duty to be virtuous or to judge the virtues and failings of others. It is a claim that emphatically calls for defence, and it is hard to see what that defence could be unless it were conducted within the terms of moral debate. No historian takes himself or his procedures outside the realm of moral judgement by the simple trick of announcing morality not to be his business. All historians judge, though some judge more accurately than others. Acton's morality of history has the enormous virtue of a system overtly declared. His claim is to be judicial, and to exercise the scruples of a judiciary. 'History deals considerably with hanging matter', he once wrote, 'and nobody ought to hang on damaged testimony'.[12] His cards lie on the table, face up, to be estimated at their true worth. In the very title of his projected history he offered a view of what human destiny is ultimately about. If he was mistaken, it does not identify his mistake to protest that morality is not the business of the historian.

Morality, after all, is not the prerogative of the ideologue, and men of cautious judgement and pragmatic interests can concern themselves as much as any speculative thinker with the problems it poses. Nor was Acton in any way alone in his age in the exacting professional demands he made upon himself. Some of the seeming oddity of his doctrine may look less odd if compared with the convictions of an eminent contemporary historian of native stock. William Stubbs, in his Oxford inaugural of 1867, eloquently demonstrated how the new ideal of critical scholarship can coexist with high moral fervour in the mind of the academic historian. The task of the new history, he told his audience, was to complete the task of the older English historians by matching 'the great German hive of historical workers' now busy in their archives, and to build 'not upon Hallam, and Palgrave, and Kemble, and Froude, and Macaulay, but on the abundant, collected, and arranged materials on which those writers tried to build whilst they were scanty, and scattered, and in disorder'. But the new German method, as Stubbs could see as clearly as Acton, in no way took history out of morality, since morality is itself knowledge; and he urged the coming generation of Oxford historians to teach

> that a multitude of half believers can never make faith; that argument never convinces any man against his will; that silence is not acquiescence; that the course of this world is anything but even and uniform; . . . that no material success, no energy of development, no eventual progress or consolidation, can atone for the mischief done by one act of falsehood, treachery, or cruelty.

All this represents a more practical and immediate morality than Acton's, and Stubbs is eager to meet the objection that his lessons are already truisms to most of those who hear them: 'Yes, but there are no truisms in facts: there are no truths which may not be stated as truisms, but there are no truths which a sound judgment can be warranted in despising.' [13]

Since no fact is a truism, any fact may be surprising; and moral purpose and the accumulation of evidence are in no sense at variance in the new Victorian school of history. 'There are no truisms in facts'; the historian might well pride himself in his capacity to wonder at the variety of man's nature, the vicissitudes of his fortune and the extremities of his moral being. That is what it is like to take a just pride in history, in its power to teach and to astonish, to question common assumption and overturn preconceptions too easily held. It is the historical subjectivist, by contrast, who is easily bored; the prophets of environment and conditioning who often assure us, in assumed tones of worldly wisdom, that everything happens as it must, that men only believe because of the circumstances of their upbringing, that the winner could never have lost or the loser ever have won. That school of assumed wisdom, which unites so much of conservative, positivist and socialist thinking, always seemed to Acton philosophically bankrupt and morally evasive. It could excuse anything, as he saw it, even the history of the popes or the philosophy of Machiavelli. 'Mobility in the moral code, subjection of man to environment, indefinite allowance for date and race, are standing formulas from Schlegel to the realistic philosophy.' [14] Despising determinism as he did, these were doctrines he dedicated his life to demolishing. History is chance, in its causative relations, and he was fond of citing the nose of Cleopatra, the grain of sand that makes a pearl in the oyster, or Napoleon's failure to dictate peace to Europe after Dresden. 'The wind saves England so often,' he remarks in a note. Man is a free being in his nature, however beset by circumstance, and his being is ultimately undetermined and swayed by hazard.

★

But two fundamental difficulties haunted Acton's great design and inhibited its progress. One is a difficulty that all such history is liable to – all projects that prefer problems to periods or concepts to events. It is the problem of delimitation. Acton is the supreme conceptual historian in the British tradition; it was a demand he made upon himself throughout his professional career, and often urged upon others. But in the case of a history of liberty it gave rise to greater difficulties than he can have considered. If all human history is the story of liberty, then a history of liberty threatens to comprehend the whole of human history. It is unthinkable without its contrary, which is tyranny; and it must pay due attention to its first and faltering pioneers such as the ancient Athenians, certain medieval scholastics, and the English Whigs – or its evolutionary struggle towards the light will be lost to view. The mass of Acton's notes show he was not the man to solve this problem by the only solution available to the historian: to stop reading, come what may, and start writing. 'The study of history', as one of his notes reads, is 'better than [the] writing of history. The writer sacrifices so much for effect.' No doubt; though making an effect is what writing is for, and the hesitation looks over-fastidious. At one point in his notes he seriously considered adding a history of conscience to his great plan, and one senses a design widening dizzyingly towards infinity. There was, after all, no compelling reason why he should ever stop reading, or stop reflecting on what he had just read. The example is everlastingly cautionary.

The other difficulty relates to Acton's highly individual view of the hundred years of Western history before his day. Two vast events overshadowed his own century from the preceding one: the American Revolution of 1776 and the French of 1789. It was not only the common apprehension of human nature they had changed, and forever, but the role of the historian as well. Acton's extreme view of this dilemma was that they had left the historian little or no place to stand. 'The triumph of the Revolutionist annuls the historian', he told his Cambridge audience hyperbolically in his inaugural of 1895, when hopes of composing his masterpiece had faded. Without those two events, the history of liberty could have been seen as a seamless web, convulsions such as 1689 only serving to restore a continuity threatened by tyrants. But continuity could be claimed for the American Revolution only with difficulty, and for the French hardly at all. 1776, as he remarks in his notes, was 'the saddest day in English history', since it represented an abandonment of law and constitutional change in favour of abstract principle:

Legally, the case of the Americans was not quite firm. Mansfield denied, Burke hesitated to affirm it. But Chatham, fed by Locke, looked beyond the letter of the law. That is why America spoke so universally.

Both revolutions were attempts to 'escape from history' and create a new order. The historian's art in tracing such connections could not easily recover from these events, as Acton conceived them, and they threatened to reduce him to the role of a wondering bystander.

A bystander, some would say, is just what the historian necessarily is, and he is often enough even less than that: one who observes and interprets events from the reports of bystanders, recording and speculating at two or more removes. That was not Acton's aspiration. The historian does not merely report and represent the deeds of others, in his view, but attempts himself to act. He aspires to influence present and future through chronicling and interpreting the past. That claim, large as it sounds, is powerful in Gladstonian Liberalism, and it helps to explain the double working life of a Prime Minister who shared his public cares with an active interest in the Homeric controversy. Acton is the historian at Gladstone's elbow, and his history would have justified the policies of his master through an interpretation of the human past. 'Liberalism is not only a principle of government', he wrote, 'but a philosophy of history.' The historic task of the Liberal had been to admit 'the dominion of conscience' into public affairs, and Acton's purpose was to trace that permeating influence in British institutions since the Stuarts, along with its ultimate sources and future hopes. A 'theory of liberalism as the unity of history' is the task he set himself, 'to be carefully worked out'. And permeation, not utopia, was his model of political advance. Progress, he wrote to Mary Gladstone in 1884, 'depends not only on the victory, the uncertain and intermittent victory, of Liberals over Conservatives, but the permeation of Conservatism with Liberal ideas, the successive conversion of Tory leaders. . . .'[15]

That such progress could be frustrated by revolution was a bitter truth, and one he felt more deeply than the issue required. Like George Orwell half a century later, he could see with clarity that it is reform that changes and revolution that maintains: that is why the true radical truly hates revolution. The paradox of conservative revolution, which had already been played out in Europe by the two Napoleons and has since been exemplified in many nations in

Europe and beyond, was actively present to his mind. 'The object of Revolution is the prevention of Revolution', he once noted; no government is more adamant in disallowing opposition and protest than one established by a violent convulsion that denies the past. The prospect darkened his thought, as well it might, menacing the entire fabric of historical continuity through change. It was an intelligent fear, as the years since his death have shown. But it need not have created so deep a silence or so wide a gap as the empty canvas of his unwritten masterpiece.

Notes and References

The place of publication is London, unless otherwise indicated after the short title.

1 THE NEW LEFT

1. Marx's early writings were first published in the *Marx–Engels Gesamtausgabe* (Berlin, 1932), and the first English version, by Martin Milligan, appeared in Moscow in 1960. The acquaintance of the British New Left with these documents seems to have been no earlier than that; see Raymond Williams, 'The Future of Marxism', *Twentieth Century* (July 1961), who welcomed them only coolly: 'The independent Marxists of the West have been turning, recently, to the early thought of Marx, in particular to the concept of "alienation". . . . I cannot say that I myself find in early Marx anything more than a series of brilliant hints and guesses, but I may be wrong. . . .'

2. Kenneth Tynan, *Curtains* (1961) p. 390.

3. Alasdair MacIntyre, in *Out of Apathy*, ed. E. P. Thompson (1960) p. 195.

4. See William Frank Thompson, *There Is a Spirit in Europe: a Memoir*, ed. his father and brother (1947), a posthumous collection.

5. Christopher Hill, reported in *The Times* (23 April 1957).

6. *The Gryphon* (University of Leeds, February 1937). The letter is dated 26 January 1937, when Hoggart was an eighteen-year-old freshman, and is signed 'H. R. H.', which may stand for Herbert Richard Hoggart.

7. Will Gallacher, reported in *Cambridge Review* (26 January 1940).

8. *Cambridge Review* (1 March 1940).

9. Williams, 'The Future of Marxism', *Twentieth Century* (July 1961).

10. *May Day Manifesto,* ed. Raymond Williams (Harmondsworth, 1968) p. 86.

11. Ibid., p. 88.

12. Ibid., p. 89.

13. Williams, 'The Future of Marxism', *Twentieth Century* (July 1961).

14. See *Authors Take Sides on Vietnam,* ed. Cecil Woolf and John Bagguley (1967), which published the results of a literary question-naire after the manner of *Authors Take Sides on the Spanish War,* ed. Auden *et al.* (*Left Review,* 1937).

15. See, for example, Peter Wollen, *Signs and Meanings in the Cinema: Sociology and Semiology* (1969), edited by Wollen for the British Film Institute.

16. Edward Thompson, *New Left Review* (May–June 1961). See also his review of Raymond Williams, *The Country and the City, New York Review of Books* (6 February 1975), which again complains of a lack of crispness and the burden of a 'portentous' style.

17. E. P. Thompson, 'An Open Letter to Leszek Kolakowski', *Socialist Register* (1973) 94.

18. Richard Hoggart, 'Teaching with Style', in *Of Books and Humankind,* ed. John Butt (1964); reprinted in Hoggart, *Speaking to Each Other* (1970) vol. 2.

2   GEORGE ORWELL

1. *The Collected Essays, Journalism and Letters of George Orwell,* ed. Sonia Orwell and Ian Angus, 4 vols (1968). Numerals in this chapter refer to this edition. The contents of the Penguin reprint (4 vols, 1970) are similar, though the pagination differs.

3   DID STALIN DUPE THE INTELLECTUALS?

1. Bertrand Russell, *The Practice and Theory of Bolshevism* (1920) pp. 8–9.

2. Ibid., pp. 27–8.

3. Ibid., p. 35.

4. H. G. Wells, *Russia in the Shadows* (1920) p. 64.

5. John Middleton Murry, *The Necessity of Communism* (1932) pp. 11–12.

6. Kingsley Martin, preface to *Low's Russian Sketchbook* (1932) p. 8.

7. Sidney and Beatrice Webb, *Soviet Communism: a New Civilisation?*

(1935) pp. 584–5.

8. Konradin Hobhouse, *Manchester Guardian* (4 February 1958).

9. Stephen Spender, *Forward from Liberalism* (1937) p. 260.

10. Ibid., p. 261.

11. Ibid., p. 281.

12. Ibid., pp. 293–4.

13. Michael Roberts, in preface to his anthology *New Country* (1933). Roberts had been expelled from the Communist Party in the Twenties.

14. C. Day Lewis, ibid., pp. 28–34.

15. Ibid., p. 226.

16. Charles Madge, ibid., p. 232.

17. Stephen Spender, *Trial of a Judge* (1938) p. 107.

18. T. C. Worsley, *Flannelled Fool* (1967) p. 98.

19. George Orwell, 'Inside the Whale'; reprinted in *The Collected Essays, Journalism and Letters of George Orwell,* ed. Sonia Orwell and Ian Angus (1968) vol. I, p. 516.

20. C. Day Lewis, *Left Review*, no. 2 (1934). The phrase 'feel small' is quoted by P. Wyndham Lewis in his novel *The Revenge for Love* (1937) v, 2, where a Communist character is shown as trained in cold-blooded tactics and devoted to Machiavelli's *Prince*.

21. C. Day Lewis, *The Buried Day* (1960) p. 129

22. Arthur Koestler, *The Invisible Writing* (1954) p. 389.

23. John Middleton Murry, 'Communism and the Universities', *Oxford Outlook* (May 1932).

24. Quoted in W. T. McKinnon, *Apollo's Blended Dream: a Study of the Poetry of Louis MacNeice* (Oxford, 1971) pp. 31–2.

25. Stephen Spender, *World within World* (1951) p. 262.

26. Ibid., p. 247.

27. W. H. Auden *et al., I Believe* (1939) p. 31.

28. David Caute, *The Fellow-Travellers* (1973) p. 174.

29. Monroe K. Spears, *The Poetry of W. H. Auden* (New York, 1963) p. 86.

30. *Poetry of the Thirties,* ed. Robin Skelton (Harmondsworth, 1964) p. 41.

31. Copyright 1977 by the estate of W. H. Auden; printed by permission.

32. A. L. Rowse, *Politics and the Younger Generation* (1931) pp. 83–4.

33. Michael Ayrton, letter to Kingsley Martin of December 1966; quoted in C. H. Rolph, *Kingsley: the Life, Letters and Diaries of Kingsley*

Martin (1973) pp. 208–9.

34. Louis MacNeice, *The Strings Are False* (1965) p. 146.

35. Dr Edith Summerskill, in *Britain and the Soviets: Congress of Peace and Friendship with the USSR 1935* (1936) p. 151.

36. Maurice Dobb, *Russia To-day and To–morrow* (1930) pp. 32–3.

37. Christopher Caudwell, *Romance and Realism* (Princeton, 1970) pp. 134–5, from a manuscript written in 1935–6.

38. Christopher Isherwood, *Mr Norris Changes Trains* (1935) ch. 5.

39. G. Bernard Shaw, notes reproduced in manuscript facsimile in Allan Chappelow, *Shaw: 'the Chucker-out'* (1969) p. 233.

40. John Strachey, *The Theory and Practice of Socialism* (1936) p. 409.

4   THE LITERATURE OF FASCISM

1. P. Wyndham Lewis, in *Enemy*, no. 3 (1928).

2. Sir J. A. R. Marriott, *The Makers of Modern Italy* (Oxford, 1931) p. 198. Marriott (1859–1945), a popular historian, had been a Conservative M.P. from 1917 to 1929. He did not alter his eulogy of Mussolini in a corrected reprint of 1937.

3. Christopher Isherwood, *Lions and Shadows* (1938) p. 73, describing his Cambridge freshman year of 1923–4.

4. W. H. Auden, *The Dance of Death* (1933) p. 17.

5. Ronald Schuchard, 'T. S. Eliot as an Extension Lecturer 1916–19', *Review of English Studies*, new ser., XXV (1974).

6. Harold Nicolson, *Diaries and Letters 1930–9*, ed. Nigel Nicolson (1966) p. 106, from an entry of 6 January 1932.

7. W. Horsfall Carter, 'Fascism as a World Force', *New English Weekly* (13 October 1932).

8. Isherwood, *Lions and Shadows*, pp. 78–9.

9. Sir Ernest Barker, *Oliver Cromwell and the English People* (Cambridge, 1937) p. 78. The Epilogue was written on his return to England.

10. Ibid., p. 82.

11. Ibid., pp. 95–6.

12. Hilaire Belloc, 1937 introduction to *The Jews* (first published in 1922) p. xxvi.

13. Ibid., p. xxxvi.

14. Ibid., p. xlv.

15. Ezra Pound, *The Spirit of Romance* (1910) p. 33.

16. P. Wyndham Lewis, *The Art of Being Ruled* (1926) p. 369.

17. Ezra Pound, *Guide to Kulchur* (1938) p. 95.

18. Pound, quoted by Michael Reck in 'A Conversation between Ezra Pound and Allen Ginsburg', *Evergreen Review* (June 1968). See also Mary de Rachewiltz, *Discretions* (1971), where Pound's daughter reports how, near the end of his life, he was 'plagued by all kinds of remorse', and regretted bitterly his neglect of Eliot's advice (p. 306).

19. From a letter of W. B. Yeats to Olivia Shakespear, in his *Letters*, ed. Allan Wade (1954) pp. 811–12.

20. Ibid., p. 813.

21. T. S. Eliot, 'The Literature of Fascism', *Criterion* (December 1928) 287–8, 290.

22. Ibid., 682.

23. Ibid., 690.

24. *Criterion* (October 1923) 104.

25. T. S. Eliot, *The Literature of Politics* (Conservative Political Centre, 1955) pp, 15–16.

26. P. Wyndham Lewis, *Blasting and Bombardiering* (1937) p. 17.

27. T. E. Hulme, *The Commentator* (1911); see Wallace Martin, 'Hulme: a Bibliographical Note', *Notes and Queries* (August 1962).

28. T. E. Hulme, *Speculations* (1924) p. 47.

29. Ibid., p. 57.

30. Ibid., p. 118.

31. Ibid., p. 242.

32. Ezra Pound, *Jefferson and/or Mussolini* (1935), a book written by February 1933 and, according to Pound's note, refused by forty publishers.

33. Evelyn Waugh, *Waugh in Abyssinia* (1936) p. 253.

34. Roy Campbell, *Flowering Rifle: a Poem from the Battlefield of Spain* (1939), author's note.

35. T. S. Eliot, *Criterion* (April 1934).

36. Evelyn Waugh, *Robbery under Law* (1939) pp. 16–17.

5 LEFT AND RIGHT

1. John Bowle, *Viscount Samuel: a Biography* (1957) p. 280.

2. *New* (later *Oxford*) *English Dictionary* (*O.E.D.*) of 1908, under 'left' (2c). In an earlier volume of 1895, the Dictionary had already specified 'the French Chamber' of Deputies as being an amphitheatre, implying that spatial terms could not apply to the

rectangular chambers at Westminster, and justifying all such terms by the seating of the French National Assembly after 1789.

3. *O.E.D. Supplement* (Oxford, 1933). For some exceptional uses of Left and Right by Victorians, including Walter Bagehot, Mark Pattison and even Gladstone, see George Watson, *The English Ideology* (1973) pp. 93ff. and Elizabeth Gaskell, *Letters* (Manchester, 1966) p. 60.

4. See Geoffrey Lloyd, 'Right and Left in Greek Philosophy', in *Right & Left*, ed. Rodney Needham (Chicago, 1973), a collection of anthropological essays.

5. Letter by George Orwell of 1949, in *The Collected Essays, Journalism and Letters of George Orwell*, ed. Sonia Orwell and Ian Angus (1968) vol. IV, p. 496.

6. Ibid., vol. III, p. 74; from *The Lion and the Unicorn* (1941).

7. Ibid., vol. II, p. 63; from an article in *Tribune* (24 December 1943).

8. The Left Book Club was founded in May 1936 and reached a climax of 57,000 members in 1939; see John Lewis, *The Left Book Club: an Historical Record* (1970).

9. See T. S. Eliot's letter to the editor, *Times Literary Supplement* (9 August 1957).

10. Edgar Foxall, 'A Note on Working-Class Solidarity', reprinted in *Poetry of the Thirties*, ed. Robin Skelton (Harmondsworth, 1964) p. 66.

11. Evelyn Waugh, *A Little Learning* (1964) p. 1.

12. Roy Campbell, *Light on a Dark Horse* (1951) ch. 22.

13. *Die Rote Fahne* (September 1930), reprinted in *Komintern und Faschismus*, ed. Theo Pirker (Stuttgart, 1965) p. 156.

14. H. J. Laski, *The Rise of European Liberalism* (1936) p. 251.

15. See Ezra Pound, *What Is Money For?* (1939), where he quotes approvingly from Lenin, Hitler, Mussolini and C. H. Douglas in his attack on usury; *Selected Prose 1909–65*, ed. William Cookson (1973) pp. 268–9.

16. P. Wyndham Lewis, *The Hitler Cult* (1939) p. 117.

17. Sir Oswald Mosley, *My Life* (1968) p. 318 note, objecting to John Harrison, *The Reactionaries* (1966), a self-righteous account of the political views of Yeats, Eliot, Pound, Wyndham Lewis and D. H. Lawrence.

18. Cesare Foligno, *SPE Tract*, no. XIX (Oxford, 1925) pp. 29–31.

19. *New English Weekly* (28 April 1932), from an anonymous

book-review. Mussolini had 'tried to create a Socialist Italy as a fiat', wrote the reviewer, 'and failed because the people do not want Socialism'.

20. W. Horsfall Carter, *Fortnightly Review* (September 1932); quoted in Vernon Bartlett, *Nazi Germany Explained* (1933) ch. 8. Bartlett himself saw National Socialism as primarily 'a reaction against excessive materialism', and compares Hitler, who 'believes in sincerity' above everything, with Gandhi (p. 73).

21. From D. H. Lawrence's introduction to Dostoevsky, *The Grand Inquisitor* (1930); reprinted in his *Phoenix* (1936) p. 285.

22. Robert Graves, *Contemporary Techniques of Poetry* (1925) pp. 42–3.

23. *Komintern und Faschismus,* ed. Pirker (1965) p. 151.

24. Quoted by Roy Harrod, *The Life of John Maynard Keynes* (1951) p. 462.

25. *Poetry of the Thirties,* ed. Robin Skelton, p. 41. See also Pound's Foreword to his *Selected Prose 1909–65,* ed. W. Cookson (1973), written in the last weeks of his life: '*Re* usury: I was out of focus, taking a symptom for a cause. The cause is AVARICE.'

6   THE MYTH OF CATASTROPHE

1. George Orwell, *The Collected Essays, Journalism and Letters,* ed. Sonia Orwell and Ian Angus (1968) vol. II, p. 392, from Orwell's war diary of April 1941, recalling events of the previous September; vol. II, pp. 78, 424.

2. F. Scott Fitzgerald, *Letters,* ed. Andrew Turnbull (1963) pp. 289–90, from a letter of 6 June 1940.

3. Frank Kermode, 'The Modern Apocalypse', ch. 4 of his *The Sense of an Ending* (1966).

4. Frank Kermode, 'D. H. Lawrence and the Apocalyptic Types' (1967), reprinted in his *Continuities* (1968) and in his *Modern Essays* (1971).

·5. C. H. Rolph, *Kingsley: the Life, Letters and Diaries of Kingsley Martin* (1973) p. 206.

6. Orwell, *Collected Essays* (1968) vol. II, p. 277.

7. A. J. P. Taylor, *English History 1914–45* (Harmondsworth, 1970) p. 236.

8. Scott Fitzgerald, *Letters,* pp. 289–90, from a letter of 6 June 1940.

9. Orwell, *Collected Essays* (1968) vol. II, p. 14; from *New English Weekly* (21 March 1940).

7 THE POLITICS OF D. H. LAWRENCE

1. Bertrand Russell, *Autobiography* (1967–9) vol. II, p. 21.

2. The Epilogue was excluded from the first edition by the Oxford University Press as unsuitable for a school text; it remained unpublished until the new edition of 1971.

3. Russell, *Autobiography*, vol. II, p. 22.

4. *New Statesman* (13 October 1934); reprinted in *Phoenix* (1936), which suggests 1924, however, as the date of composition (p. 839).

5. J. D. Chambers, preface to 1965 edition of Jessie Chambers, *D. H. Lawrence: a Personal Record* (1965) p. xv.

6. J. D. Chambers, 'Memories of D. H. Lawrence', *Renaissance and Modern Studies*, XVI (1972).

7. Harry T. Moore, *The Intelligent Heart: the Story of D. H. Lawrence* (revised 1960) p. 116.

8. Helen Corke, *In Our Infancy: an Autobiography 1882–1912* (Cambridge, 1975) p. 166.

9. *Phoenix II*, ed. Harry T. Moore (1968) p. 560.

10. Lady Cynthia Asquith, *Diaries 1915–18* (1968) pp. 18–19.

11. *D. H. Lawrence: the Critical Heritage*, ed. R. P. Draper (1970) pp. 322ff.

12. Stephen Potter, *D. H. Lawrence: a First Study* (1930) pp. 9–10.

13. John Middleton Murry, *Son of Woman* (1931) p. 24.

14. William Empson, *Some Versions of Pastoral* (1935) pp. 7–8.

15. Christopher Caudwell, *Studies in a Dying Culture* (1938) p. 57.

16. F. R. Leavis, 'Keynes, Lawrence and Cambridge', *Scrutiny*, XVI (1949); reprinted in his *Common Pursuit* (1952) p. 258.

17. *Collected Letters of D. H. Lawrence*, ed. Harry T. Moore (New York, 1962) vol. II, p. 1110, from a letter of 28 December 1928.

18. Richard Hoggart, *The Uses of Literacy* (1957) ch. 2, section C.

19. Raymond Williams, *Culture and Society 1780–1950* (1958) ch. 3, section 1.

20. Helen Corke, *In Our Infancy*, reports that on country walks 'his talk is like an appendix to *The White Peacock*' (p. 179).

21. Edith Sitwell, *Taken Care of* (1965) p. 108.

22. 'Autobiographical Sketch' first published in *Lawrence: a Composite Biography*, ed. Edward Nehls (Madison, 1957–9) vol. III, pp. 300–2; reprinted in *Phoenix II*, ed. Harry T. Moore (1968).

23. Richard Aldington, *D. H. Lawrence* (1930) pp. 21–2.

24. Quoted in Moore, *The Intelligent Heart*, p. 439.

25. J. D. Chambers, 'Memories of D. H. Lawrence', *Renaissance and Modern Studies*, XVI (1972).

8 RACE AND THE SOCIALISTS

1. See, for instance, Edmund Silberner, *The Anti-Semitic Tradition in Modern Socialism* (Jerusalem, 1953) and *Sozialisten zur Judenfrage* (Berlin, 1962); George Lichtheim, 'Socialism and the Jews', *Dissent* (New York, July–August 1968), mainly on nineteenth-century France; Robert S. Wistrich, 'Karl Marx and the Jewish Question', *Soviet Jewish Affairs*, IV (1974); J. M. Winter, 'The Webbs and the Non-White World', *Journal of Contemporary History*, IX (1974); and W. H. Chaloner and W. O. Henderson, 'Marx/Engels and Racism', *Encounter* (November 1975).

2. For example, Christine Bolt, *Victorian Attitudes to Race* (1971), abundantly documented as it is from periodicals and travel literature, glibly assumes that all racial theories are mere prejudice or 'primitive superstition', that the word 'race' always refers to genetic difference, even before the twentieth century, and that racialism is essentially right-wing.

3. See my account of the 'bright' side of Victorian racial ideas in *The English Ideology* (1973) pp. 205ff.

4. See William Oddie, 'Dickens and the Indian Mutiny', *Dickensian*, LXVIII (1972); Harry Stone, 'Dickens and the Jews', *Victorian Studies*, II (1959); George Ford, 'The Governor Eyre Case in England', *University of Toronto Quarterly*, XVII (1948); and K. J. Fielding, '*Edwin Drood* and Governor Eyre', *Listener* (25 December 1952). The problem was first exposed, and the Dickens–Davis correspondence first published, in Cumberland Clark, *Charles Dickens and his Jewish Characters* (1918).

5. See Walter L. Arnstein, *The Bradlaugh Case* (Oxford, 1965) pp. 66, 198. The first Jew, religiously speaking, elected to the Commons was the Baron de Rothschild in 1847, but he had to wait for eleven years before a relief Bill gave him the right to speak or vote.

6. *The Times* (1 December 1888); R. P. Masani, *Dadabhai Naoroji* (1939) pp. 263ff. But Salisbury is not a serious candidate for racialism; in the following year he convened the Anti-Slave-Trade Conference in Brussels, and told a City audience in November, 1889 how, at British insistence, both Zanzibar and Egypt had begun to

resist slavery and slave-hunting. Ten years later, in a letter of 8 June 1900, he attacked the arrogance of the 'damned nigger' elements in British society in Bombay as both 'offensive and unworthy', and as constituting a 'serious political danger'; see J. A. S. Grenville, *Lord Salisbury and Foreign Policy* (1964) p. 295.

7. *Nation* (28 April 1928), reviewing W. T. J. Gun, *Studies in Hereditary Ability*. The review is reprinted in J. M. Keynes, *Essays in Biography*, ed. Geoffrey Keynes (1951) p. 68. For more Cambridge Kingsman gossip, this time laced with academic sociology, see Noel Annan, 'The Intellectual Aristocracy', in *Studies in Social History: a Tribute to G. M. Trevelyan* (1955).

8. Robert Payne, *The Unknown Karl Marx: Documents* (New York, 1971) pp. 14–15. David McLellan, in *Marx before Marxism* (1970), denies that Marx's early essays give grounds for calling him anti-Jewish, though it is important to remember that it was possible to be that without being a racialist. I can find no clear evidence to support his contention that 'Judenthum' had 'very little religious, and still less racial, content' for Marx (p. 142).

9. Marx, *The Eastern Question*, ed. Eleanor Marx and Edward Aveling (1897) p. 60.

10. Marx and Engels, *Werke* (East Berlin, 1964) vol. XXX, p. 259.

11. I am indebted to Mr Trevor Jones, editor of *Harrap's Standard German and English Dictionary*, for this detail. Marx had already used the word 'nigger' in quotation five years before, with indignation, in an article in the *New York Daily Tribune* on the Indian Mutiny (4 September 1857); see Marx and Engels, *The First Indian War of Independence* (Moscow, 1960) p. 93. 'Nigger' is recorded by *O.E.D.* as in use as early as 1786.

12. First collected in *Aus dem literarischen Nachlass von Marx, Engels und Lassalle*, ed. Franz Mehring (Stuttgart, 1902) vol. III, pp. 236ff., and translated in *The Russian Menace to Europe: a Collection of Articles, Speeches, Letters and News Dispatches*, ed. P. W. Blackstock and Bert F. Hoselitz (1953) pp. 61ff.

13. *The Ethnological Notebooks of Karl Marx*, ed. Lawrence Krader (Assen, 1972, for the International Institute of Social History).

14. Marx and Engels, *Werke*, vol. XXX, p. 578, from a letter of January 1861.

15. *Das Kapital* (1914 edition) vol. I, p. 306.

16. *Ethnological Notebooks*, pp. 115, 127.

17. Ibid., p. 292.

18. Ibid., pp. 74–5, from Krader's introduction.

19. Beatrice Webb, *My Apprenticeship* (1926) p. 61.

20. Havelock Ellis, *The Task of Social Hygiene* (1912) p. 402.

21. H. G. Wells, *Anticipations* (1902) p. 317.

22. H. G. Wells, *The Science of Life* (1929–30) IX, i, 3.

23. J. B. S. Haldane, *The Inequality of Man* (1932) p. 24.

24. Translated from the report of the judicial hearing in *Frankfurter Allgemeine Zeitung* (15 December 1972).

9 THE SOCIAL CRITICISM OF MATTHEW ARNOLD

1. Raymond Williams, *Culture and Society 1780–1950* (1958) I, vii.

2. On rivalry between poets and novelists, see Peter Conrad, *The Victorian Treasure-House* (1973) ch. 6.

3. Adam Smith, *The Wealth of Nations* (1776) bk iv, ch. 9.

4. *London Review* (13 February 1869); *Athenaeum* (20 February 1869). I am indebted for some of these references to an unpublished doctoral thesis in the University of London by S. Sengupta (1961).

5. Florence E. Hardy, *The Early Life of Thomas Hardy* (1928) p. 175.

6. *The Times* (13 November 1886); reprinted in *Matthew Arnold: Essays, Letters and Reviews,* ed. Fraser Neiman (Cambridge, Mass., 1960) p. 308.

7. *Letters of Matthew Arnold 1848–88.* ed. G. W. E. Russell (1895) vol. II, p. 9, from a letter to his mother of 5 June 1869: 'My chance of a commissionership under William's Bill [the Endowed Schools Act of 1869] seems small, Gladstone stopping the way. This is natural enough. . . .'

8. Gillian Sutherland, *Policy-Making in Elementary Education 1870-95* (Oxford, 1973) comments: 'There is nothing to compare with this series of elegant begging letters from any one of the other Inspectors' (p. 61 and note). See also her introduction to the Penguin selection, *Matthew Arnold on Education* (Harmondsworth, 1973). I am grateful for Mrs Sutherland's information, and especially for guiding my attention to manuscript materials listed in the appendix to this chapter.

9. James Runciman, *Schools and Scholars* (1887) p. 164.

10. *A. E. Housman: Selected Prose,* ed. John Carter (Cambridge, 1961) pp. 197-8, from a paper of the 1890s, where Housman hails Arnold as 'the great critic of our land and time'.

11. Rupert Brooke, *Democracy and the Arts* (1946) p. 32.

12. Ezra Pound, *The Spirit of Romance* (1910) p. 234 note.

10   ACTON'S 'HISTORY OF LIBERTY'

1. Mary Drew (formerly Gladstone), *Acton, Gladstone and Others* (1924) p. 7.

2. Acton, *Selections from the Correspondence*, ed. J. N. Figgis and R. V. Laurence (1917) vol. I, p. 7.

3. Acton, *The History of Freedom and Other Essays* (1907) p. 432.

4. *Letters of Lord Acton to Mary Gladstone*, ed. Herbert Paul (1904) p. 174.

5. *Lord Acton and his Circle*, ed. Abbot Gasquet (1906) p. 13.

6. *Bridgnorth Journal* (3 March 1877). The second lecture was reported there on 2 June 1877. Both are reprinted in the posthumous *History of Freedom and Other Essays* (1907), along with the review of Erskine May.

7. Principally Cambridge University Library Add. MSS. 4937–56, 5442, in twenty-one boxes and comprising over six thousand notes, though the dimensions of the 'History of Liberty' are not always easy to discern among his other notes. Most of them date from 1877–83. I am deeply grateful to St John's College, Cambridge, for aid in having these notes transcribed, and to the patience of Mrs P. Parsons in transcribing them. See John Loose, 'A Guide to the Acton Papers in Cambridge University Library' (typed copy in University Library, 1971).

8. *Selections from the Correspondence*, vol. I, p. 33.

9. *Letters to Mary Gladstone*, p. 60, from a letter of January 1881.

10. James Bryce, *Studies in Contemporary Biography* (1903) pp. 396–7.

11. Geoffrey Elton, introduction to J. N. Figgis, *The Divine Right of Kings* (New York, 1965); reprinted in Elton, *Studies in Tudor and Stuart Politics and Government* (Cambridge, 1974) vol. II, p. 195.

12. Acton, *Historical Essays & Studies* (1907) p. 353.

13. William Stubbs, *An Address Delivered by Way of Inaugural Lecture* (Oxford, 1867) pp. 18–19, 27–8.

14. Acton, *Historical Essays & Studies*, p. 355.

15. *Letters to Mary Gladstone*, p. 200.

Index